JODY DAVIS • JOHNNY KLING • BOB SCHEFFING

GRACE • BILL BUCKNER • RYNE SANDBERG • BILLY

HORNSBY • BILLY JURGES • DON KESSINGER • JOE

CK • ARAMIS RAMIREZ • NED ... N • WOODY

J • GARY MATTHEWS • RIGGS STEPHENSON • HACK

WILDFIRE SCHULTE • SAMMY SOSA • ANDRE DAWSON

YLER • MIKE "KING" KELLY • FERGUSON JENKINS •

UX • KERRY WOOD • RICK SUTCLIFFE • KENNY

• LARRY FRENCH • JACK PFIESTER • BRUCE SUTTER

N • LEO DUROCHER • DON ZIMMER • DUSTY BAKER

• RANDY HUNDLEY • JODY DAVIS • JOHNNY KLING •

VARRETTA • MARK GRACE • BILL BUCKNER • RYNE

Y EVERS • ROGERS HORNSBY • BILLY JURGES • DON

HACK • BILL MADLOCK • ARAMIS RAMIREZ • NED

K SAUER • MOISES ALOU • GARY MATTHEWS • RIGGS

NDAY • CY WILLIAMS • WILDFIRE SCHULTE • SAMMY

ZEN SHIRLEY "KIKI" CUYLER • MIKE "KING" KELLY •

ROWN • GREG MADDUX • KERRY WOOD • RICK

GHN • DICK ELLSWORTH • LARRY FRENCH • JACK

FEW AND CHOSEN

FEW AND CHOSEN

Defining Cubs Greatness Across the Eras

Ron Santo

with Phil Pepe

TRIUMPH
BOOKS
CHICAGO

Library of Congress Cataloging-in-Publication Data

Santo, Ron, 1940–
    Few and chosen : defining Cubs greatness across the eras / Ron Santo and Phil Pepe.
      p. cm.
    Includes index.
    ISBN 1-57243-710-3
    1. Chicago Cubs (Baseball team)—History. 2. Baseball players—Rating of. I. Pepe, Phil. II. Title.

GV875.C58S36   2005
796.357′64′0977311—dc22

                                         2004062076

This book is available in quantity at special discounts for your group or organization. For further information, contact:

Triumph Books
601 South LaSalle Street
Suite 500
Chicago, Illinois 60605
(312) 939-3330
Fax (312) 663-3557

Printed in U.S.A.
ISBN-13: 978-1-57243-710-4
ISBN-10: 1-57243-710-3
Design by Nick Panos; page production by Patricia Frey

Now it's our turn!

Boston fans waited 86 years for their Red Sox to win another World Series, but 86 years is a mere blink of an eye compared to what Chicago Cubs fans have endured. They have been waiting for 97 years, longer than any other team.

Through nearly a century of deprivation, disappointment, and despair, Cubs fans have remained steadfast, loyal, and supportive. They love their Cubs and they have demonstrated that love through thick and thin (mostly thin). That entitles them to be hailed as the greatest fans in the world.

And so this book is dedicated to those long-suffering Cubs fans, and it comes with a message of hope, borrowed from the Red Sox:

Why not us?

Why not now?

Contents

Foreword by Ernie Banks ix

Preface by Ron Santo xiii

Preface by Phil Pepe xxi

Acknowledgments.......................xxvii

Introduction by Ryne Sandberg......xxix

ONE Catcher 1

TWO First Baseman 13

THREE Second Baseman 27

FOUR Shortstop 43

FIVE Third Baseman 57

SIX Left Fielder.....................................69

SEVEN Center Fielder................................81

EIGHT Right Fielder 95

NINE Right-Handed Pitcher....................109

TEN Left-Handed Pitcher 123

ELEVEN Relief Pitcher 137

TWELVE Manager 149

THIRTEEN Team..165

Index 183

Foreword

MANY YEARS AGO, a grand old Chicago sportswriter named Jim Enright pinned the nickname "Mr. Cub" on me. I told Jim I was flattered and honored by the name, but that there should be a different "Mr. Cub" every year. At the time I said that, I was thinking about Ronnie Santo, who really was "Mr. Cub" in the sixties and seventies.

Ronnie had, and still has, all the qualities you look for in someone you would want to carry the name "Mr. Cub." As a player, he was a great competitor, a hard worker, and a leader. He had intensity. He was determined and ambitious. He wanted to win more than anybody I've ever known. He had spirit, and he still does.

I saw him through good times and bad times, when he lost his mom and dad, and recently in his battle with diabetes. I lockered right beside him for years, and I never knew he had this disease. I remember once after I found out about Ronnie's diabetes, I mentioned to him that I had a friend who had recently found out she was a diabetic. He told me to call her, and he got on the phone and talked to her and told her what she had to do. This was someone he didn't even know, but he took the time to counsel her, and his talk encouraged her and lifted her spirits.

Ronnie has handled his own ailment like the true champion he is. He's a very positive person, the most courageous person I've ever been around. I'm inspired by him and by his spirit. Ron Santo is one of my idols, one of my heroes. He's almost like an alien. He's so special it's as if he's not real. This guy is really an amazing person. I love being around him. I love the man. I love Ron Santo.

The first time I saw Santo, he was just a kid up from the minor leagues, and he joined us in Pittsburgh. It was 1960. We played the Pirates in a double-header, and Ronnie played both games and had an unbelievable day. I said to myself, this guy can really play.

The Cubs weren't very good in those days, but we slowly got better, and Ronnie was a large part of that improvement. By 1969, we were a championship-caliber team. More important, that was a special group of guys. What made us special was that we were all very close. We didn't win a pennant, but we formed friendships that are ongoing today.

People say it's a pity that I played 19 major league seasons (all of them with the Cubs, by the way) and never got into the World Series and never won anything, but I don't agree. I won a lot. I won the respect of my fans, my family, and my friends. That's real winning. That's the kind of winning that lasts a lifetime.

Just recently I played golf at Augusta National with a group of business-men, including Bill Gates, and I started thinking, "Here I am, a poor kid from Dallas, Texas, one of a family of 12, and I'm playing golf with half of the world's economy."

That was just amazing to me, and it was made possible only through my life with the Cubs.

How blessed I was to be a baseball player and to have played for the Cubs, in the city of Chicago, with the greatest fans in the world. Cubs fans are like no other fans. Well, maybe Red Sox fans are close. With Cubs fans it's a gen-erational thing. Young people come to Wrigley Field and they have never seen the Cubs win. Their parents never saw the Cubs win. Their grandparents never saw the Cubs win. Maybe their great-grandparents saw the Cubs win—the Cubs won 16 National League championships, you know. But these young people still come to Wrigley Field hoping that every year will be the year. They love their Cubs, and they're loyal despite the Cubs' not winning for so many years.

Those of us who were together for six, seven, eight years, like Billy Williams, Randy Hundley, Fergie Jenkins, Glenn Beckert, Don Kessinger, and Ron Santo, came to feel that love and that loyalty. There's nothing bet-ter than loyalty. Nothing.

After Ron Santo retired from baseball, he went into business and was very successful. Then he became a radio broadcaster on Cubs games, and he's very successful at that. The people love him because he knows the game and because he loves the Cubs as much as they do.

Now, Ronnie is an author and has written this book in which he chooses his all-time Cubs team, and I see he has picked me at two positions: first base and shortstop. That's awfully nice of him. Playing both positions, and playing them well defensively, was something I took a lot of pride in. I never wanted to be just a good offensive player. I wanted to play well on defense, too.

People are always kidding me because I like to say, "Let's play two today." Well, I meant it then, and I mean it now. Let's play two, and I'll play both games: one at first base and the other at shortstop.

—Ernie Banks

Preface

I CONSIDER MYSELF VERY FORTUNATE that I got to play most of my career with a team I love very much, the Chicago Cubs, and that I got to play home games in Wrigley Field. And I'm doubly fortunate that I'm still associated with the Cubs as a radio broadcaster.

I feel like I was born to play day baseball. I got to Chicago when I was 20 years old, and for my entire career with the Cubs, I played all my home games the way baseball was meant to be played: in daylight.

I was born and raised in Seattle, Washington—as far from Chicago as you can get and still be in the continental United States—but I consider Chicago my home: all my kids were born and raised there, and I consider the Cubs my extended family. I grew up in a section of Seattle called "Garlic Gulch," which got its name because it was an Italian-American community. My father was born in Italy, and my mother was born in Sweden. I like to say I'm half Italian, half Swedish, and all American. We weren't poor, but we were by no means rich, so I guess you could say we were middle class. Maybe lower middle class, but I never wanted for anything.

At Franklin High School in Seattle, I played baseball, basketball, and football. In football, I was all-city quarterback and I played safety on defense. I had offers to play football in college, but baseball was my first love.

As a kid, I seemed to be ahead of my time. In Little League, I was playing with 12-year-olds when I was 7. I was the second Little Leaguer to go to the big leagues; Joey Jay, who pitched for the Braves and Reds, was the first. I played Pony League baseball when I was 12, and then I played on my high school team.

In my sophomore year in high school, a local bird-dog scout for the Cubs named Dave Koescher started following me. One day, Dave told me, "You're going to be a big leaguer and you're going to hit home runs."

At the time, I wasn't very big, and I was more of a line-drive hitter. By my senior year, scouts were coming around. I had a job working for the Seattle Rainiers of the Class AAA Pacific Coast League as the clubhouse boy in Sicks Stadium, and I was selected to play in the Hearst Tournament, which was a national baseball tournament run by Hearst newspapers all over the country. I was one of 60 kids selected to play in our area, out of which they would choose a team to go to New York to play as United States All-Stars against a team of New York All-Stars.

I was named Most Valuable Player in our region and was chosen to be on the U.S. team that went to New York. We played against the New York All-Stars in the old Polo Grounds. Joe Torre was the third baseman for the New York All-Stars, and I was the catcher for the United States All-Stars. I had played third base in high school until my senior year, but when our catcher got hurt my coach put me behind the plate because I had a strong arm.

All 16 major league teams had scouts at those games in New York, and when it was over, the Yankees asked me to stay and work out at Yankee Stadium. I was a Yankees fan in those days, and my favorite player was Mickey Mantle. We had no major league baseball on the West Coast at the time, and I followed the games on television. Naturally the Yankees always played in the national *Game of the Week* because they were winning every year, and I got to be a Yankees fan.

It was tempting when the Yankees asked me to work out, but I guess I was a little homesick, so I told them, "No, I have to get back home." Who knows what might have happened if I stayed. I might have been a Yankee. But I have no regrets with how things worked out.

When I got back home, the scouts started coming around with their offers, including the Yankees. The first team that came in was the Cleveland Indians. The Indians' scout shook my hand, and he shook my dad's hand and said, "We're very interested in your son. We'd like to give him a Double A contract and a $50,000 bonus to sign."

I couldn't swallow. I was 18 years old, and $50,000 was a lot of money in 1958. I couldn't imagine having that much money. Even my dad was overwhelmed. He had a cleaning business, and it probably took him five years to make $50,000.

Cincinnati operated the Seattle team in the Pacific Coast League, so you might say they had a particular interest in signing me and might have felt they had an advantage. Dewey Soriano, the general manager of the Rainiers, said, "Son, we'd like you to put on a uniform, and we'd like to see you take batting practice."

I put on the uniform and grabbed my 31-ounce bat—I was 6' tall, 165 pounds at the time—and I stepped into the batting cage. And who was on the mound but Don Newcombe! He was rehabbing from some elbow or shoulder problem. The first pitch he got inside on me, and he broke my bat right in half. Ed Bailey threw me his bat that must have weighed 36 ounces. I was so nervous, I don't think I got one out of the cage, but Soriano came to my house with a scout, and the Reds made me the highest offer: $80,000.

The rest of the offers were all around $50,000, except for the Cubs. Dave Koescher called and said, "Ron, I know what you have been offered, but the Cubs are only going to offer $20,000." I was a little disappointed, but I liked Dave very much and he had been with me since I was a sophomore, so I felt I owed him the courtesy of at least listening to the Cubs' offer. I asked him if he was going to be involved in the discussion, and he said he was, but he had to bring along Hard Rock Johnson, who was the Cubs' chief scout.

Hard Rock walked into my home and said to my dad, "We can only offer your son $20,000, and we'll sign him only as a catcher." It was kind of a take-it-or-leave-it ultimatum, and my dad was insulted by it, but he held his tongue and shook Hard Rock's hand and thanked him for coming. Johnson was going to drive Dave back, but I told Dave, "Stick around; I'll drive you home."

Dave told me he was embarrassed by Hard Rock's attitude, but I said, "Don't worry, Dave. I haven't made a decision yet. I'm going to sit down with my dad tonight and decide."

That night, my dad and I talked over my options. My dad said, "There's two ways of looking at this. You can take the $80,000 from Cincinnati and you'll be set for life"—that's how much money $80,000 seemed to us—"or you can go with the Cubs' offer because Dave Koescher is a good man and he's believed in you from the start. It's up to you."

I told my dad there was just something about Wrigley Field that attracted me. I used to watch Cubs games on the *Game of the Week*, and I was fascinated by Wrigley Field and by Ernie Banks. As for the Cubs signing me as a catcher, in the back of my mind I always believed I would eventually play third base because that's the position I loved.

Call me crazy, but I signed with the Cubs for $20,000 and turned down the Reds' offer of $80,000. Something just told me this was the right situation for me. I can't explain it. It was the mystique of Wrigley Field, day baseball, and Ernie Banks. And one more thing! When I was 12 years old, a buddy of mine from Seattle moved to Chicago and was there for two years. When he left, we were the same size, and when he returned, he was a foot taller than me, so I got to thinking they grow them big in Chicago, and that stayed with me.

As things turned out, I never second-guessed myself about leaving $60,000 on the table. Not once. Not for a minute.

Who knows what would have happened if I had taken the Cincinnati offer? I made it to Chicago after only one year in the minor leagues, and I made it as a third baseman. I hit .325 in San Antonio, had 11 home runs, and was in the 90s in RBIs. The Cubs invited me to spring training as a nonroster player. Alvin Dark had retired, and the Cubs were looking for a third baseman. They had Frank Thomas, Sammy Drake, and Harry Bright all competing for the job. There were two weeks left, and the Dodgers were coming to Arizona to play the Cubs in exhibition games the next-to-last weekend of spring training.

Charlie Grimm, the Cubs' manager, called me into his office and said, "Son, if you do well against the Dodgers, you'll break camp with us."

Don Drysdale pitched the first game, and I was two for four against him. The next day, I got two hits off Stan Williams, and Charlie told me, "Pack your bags." I was working out with the big club, but I was living in the minor league facility, and Charlie was telling me to pack my bags, which I took to mean I was moving into the Cubs' hotel.

I went to my room and started packing, when I got a call from John Holland, the general manager of the Cubs. He said, "Meet me in Charlie Grimm's room."

I went into Grimm's room, and as soon as I walked in, I knew something was wrong. Charlie was standing and John Holland was sitting, and Holland said, "Sit down, son."

I said, "No, there's something wrong here."

Holland said, "Please, son, sit down."

I said, "I'm going to stand, and you're going to tell me what's wrong."

He said, "Well, we made a trade today. We got Don Zimmer and we gave up Ron Perranoski"—who was our best pitcher and had been my roommate at San Antonio—"and Johnny Goryl. We're going to have to send you out to Triple A."

I said, "No you're not; I quit." Then I pointed right at Grimm and said, "You lied to me, Charlie. You just told me I made the ballclub. Now you're telling me I have to go back to the minor leagues. I know I can play up here."

I was so mad, I had tears rolling down my cheeks, and I turned around and walked out. I went back to my room and called my wife—I had just gotten married—and I said, "Honey, I'm coming home. I quit. They lied to me, and I'm not going to put up with it."

There was a knock on the door. It was John Holland. He said, "Don't quit. We know you're going to be in the big leagues."

I said, "Charlie promised me I was going to be on this team. I know I can play."

Holland said, "You will be back before September, I promise you. And we'll give you a major league contract."

"I don't care about a major league contract," I said. "I care about playing."

"Please, settle down," Holland said. "Just go there. We know how good you are."

I guess Holland was convincing because I gave in and agreed to go to Triple A, Houston, Texas, until the Cubs brought me up on June 26. I joined them in Pittsburgh, and the first night I was there they put me in a room with veteran pitcher Don Elston. The next day I went to Forbes Field, the first time I had ever been in a major league ballpark. I didn't even go to the locker room; I just sat there watching Roberto Clemente and Dick Groat take batting practice. Then I went into the clubhouse and I didn't even know where my uniform was.

Lou Boudreau was the manager. He had been in the radio booth, and he and Grimm changed places. Charlie went into the booth to take Boudreau's place, and Boudreau came down from the booth to be the manager. He called me into his office and said, "You're in there today. You're hitting sixth, and you're playing both games of the doubleheader."

After batting practice, I didn't even go back into the clubhouse; I just stayed in the dugout because I wanted to hear my name being announced over the loudspeaker. Ernie Banks came out and sat next to me and said, "You nervous, kid?"

I told him I was scared to death, and Ernie just sat there talking with me to calm me down. My first time up, Bob Friend threw me a breaking ball and I backed off. Smokey Burgess was catching, and as he threw the ball back to Friend, he came up and right in my ear he said, "*That's* a major league curveball, kid."

I stepped out of the batter's box. I was so nervous. There were forty thousand people in the stands. I got back in and Friend threw me a fastball, and I lined it right back past Friend's ear into center field for a base hit. It was as if the whole world was lifted off my shoulders. I had three hits in the doubleheader and drove in five runs, and we won both games. Zimmer moved to second base, and I played the remainder of the year at third.

After I had settled in, I came to love playing in Chicago and playing in Wrigley Field. Maybe because professionally I was born and raised in day baseball, to me there's not a better life for an athlete who is raising a family. Get up in the morning, have breakfast with your family, go to the ballpark, play a game, and be home in time for dinner. It's like a nine-to-five job.

People have said that playing in the Chicago heat day after day is the reason the Cubs have not won a World Series in more than a half century. I don't agree. I always felt the heat was often an advantage for us. If Bob Gibson, who threw 96, 97 miles an hour, came to town, his fastball would be a little shorter in that heat. As a hitter, you saw the ball better; you saw the rotation of the ball in the daytime. I've always believed that.

Unfortunately, the Cubs team I joined was aging, and it wasn't very good. We were at the bottom of the league for the first few years I was there. In my first six years, we never finished higher than seventh, first in an eight-team, then a ten-team league. Leo Durocher took over as manager in 1966, and we finished tenth. But the next year, we moved up to third.

By 1969, you could see we were coming together. Ernie Banks was still there, and Billy Williams had become a star. Don Kessinger came in 1964, and the next year Glenn Beckert joined us. In 1966, we got Randy Hundley and Bill Hands in a trade with the Giants and Fergie Jenkins in a trade with the Phillies. We kind of grew up together and stayed together a long time.

I thought—and still do—that we were the best team in the National League that year and the Orioles were the best team in baseball, and the Mets beat us both. The Miracle Mets!

But our 1969 team will always have a special place in my heart and in the hearts of all Cubs fans. We went out together as a team, and after a game we would sit around the clubhouse and talk for hours. We were a very close group. Our families were close. We're still close to this day. We get together every year at Randy Hundley's Fantasy Camp in Arizona and reminisce about the good old days.

As a result, if it seems I'm partial to the guys I played with in my selections for the all-time Cubs team, I hope you will understand and forgive my bias.

I have lived in Chicago for more than 40 years and have remained close to the Cubs throughout that time. As a member of the Cubs' broadcast team, I have had the pleasure of meeting most of the great players on my list, and those I have not met—like Gabby Hartnett, Hack Wilson, Cap Anson, and Three-Finger Brown—I have read about or heard about from longtime Cubs fans.

If I failed to mention your favorite Cub, I apologize. Picking an all-time Cubs team is no easy job. The Cubs have had so many great players through the years, but to me the players who made up the 1969 team are special, and always will be, so I make no apologies for picking any of them.

—Ron Santo

Preface

IT WAS GETTING MONOTONOUS . . . AND FRUSTRATING—one team dominating, blatantly raiding its rivals of their best players, accumulating the game's biggest stars, winning year after tedious year. Two straight championships. Five in seven years. Six in eleven years.

Was this really good for baseball? How could other teams compete against a team so loaded with talent, a team with an owner possessed of an insatiable desire to win and the unlimited finances to make it happen?

Sound familiar?

No, we're not talking here about the New York Yankees of George Steinbrenner. We're talking about Chicago's entry in the National League. We're talking, believe it or not, about baseball's lovable losers, the Chicago Cubs.

Of course, any Cubs fan who witnessed such a baseball dynasty, such enormous success, such unbridled joy, would have to be 125 years old.

The Cubs (they were called the White Stockings in those days and became "Cubs" in 1907) are a charter member of the National League and the oldest continuous franchise in major league baseball. Their inception dates back to 1876, when the team's owner, William A. Hulbert, tired of chronically losing in the National Association, opened his checkbook and plucked the best players from rival teams. He grabbed, among others, Albert G. Spalding and Ross Barnes from Boston and Adrian "Cap" Anson from Philadelphia.

Outraged by such bald-faced piracy, the owners of franchises in the National Association banded together and threatened to blacklist any player who jumped to Hulbert's Chicago team. Undaunted by the threat, Hulbert simply spearheaded the formation of a new league, the eight-team National League, which debuted in 1876 with franchises in St. Louis, Hartford, Boston, Louisville, New York, Philadelphia, and Cincinnati joining the Chicago club.

The White Stockings dominated play in the National League's inaugural season with a record of 52–14, finishing six games better than St. Louis. Chicago's Ross Barnes was the league's first batting champion with a .429 average. His teammate Deacon White led the league in runs batted in with 60. And Spalding, who doubled as manager and pitcher of the White Stockings, started 60 of his team's 66 games, relieved in another, and won 47.

The White Stockings won consecutive pennants in 1880, 1881, and 1882, and again in 1885 and 1886, giving them six championships in the National League's first 11 years—baseball's first dynasty. But they would go 20 years before winning another championship, a drought that would be commonplace for faithful followers of the Cubs, who could take little solace in the fact that their beloved Cubs would win a championship in five straight decades or that when they won the National League pennant in 1945, it would be the 16th championship in their history—more than any other team in major league baseball.

The painful reality is that it is more than half a century since the Cubs played in the World Series, and almost a century since they last won one.

Despite their deprivation, the Cubs fans' loyalty and zeal is second to none, and the Cubs' history and tradition is the equal of any.

Spalding pitched the first shutout in National League history for Chicago, a 4–0 victory at Louisville on April 25, 1876. Spalding also had the first hit in franchise history.

A Cub (White Stocking), Bob Addy in 1876, is credited as the first player to slide into a base.

Chicago's Ross Barnes in 1876 hit the first National League home run.

The Cubs (White Stockings) are the only team to go through an entire season (1877) without hitting a home run.

The Cubs (White Stockings) hold the record for the most runs scored in a game, a 36–7 rout of Louisville in 1897, and the most runs scored in an inning, 18 against Detroit in 1883.

Wrigley Field is the second-oldest ballpark in major league baseball. Originally named Weeghman Park, it was built for the Chicago entry in the

Federal League in 1914, two years after Boston's Fenway Park, at a cost of $250,000 and with a seating capacity of fourteen thousand. After playing their home games at five different sites, the Cubs moved into Weeghman Park in 1916. Four years later, the name was changed to Cubs Park, and in 1926, the name was changed again, to Wrigley Field, in honor of the Cubs' owner, chewing gum magnate William Wrigley Jr.

The Cubs were the last team to play a home game at night (August 9, 1988) and the first to employ an African American as a coach (Buck O'Neill in 1962, when the Cubs had no manager but employed a "college of coaches" to run the team).

The Cubs hold the major league record for consecutive victories with 21, which they accomplished twice: first as the White Stockings in 1880 and then as the Cubs in 1935.

While that remarkable streak was unfolding, Cubs fans in and around Des Moines, Iowa, followed every game, every play on radio broadcasts described by the warm, smooth voice of a young announcer called "Dutch" Reagan, who wasn't even at the ballpark. As was the custom of the day, he would sit in a studio and re-create the play-by-play received by Western Union tele- type, using sound effects to duplicate the crack of the bat and the roar of the crowd.

Years later, I had occasion to write to celebrities for a magazine article, ask- ing them to recount their best baseball memories. One letter was sent to Pacific Palisades, to an old baseball announcer named "Dutch" Reagan. About two weeks later, much to my surprise and utter delight, I received a letter in return. It's dated July 21, 1966, and it reads as follows:

> I don't think any single incident in any of the games I broad- cast as a sports announcer impressed me so much as the last few weeks of the National League season, I believe it was '35 or '36 [Editor's note: it was 1935]. At any rate, the Chicago Cubs came to a point where their only mathematical chance for winning the pennant lay in winding up the season, 21 games in all, without a defeat. I don't think anything in baseball has ever matched that.
>
> I was broadcasting the Cubs games at the time, and as the totals started to mount, and they reached 15, and then 16, with- out a defeat, and you just couldn't believe it would happen, they

went on and finished the season winning the last 21 games without a break [actually, the Cubs won 21 straight and clinched the pennant, then lost their last two and finished four games ahead of the Cardinals]. This, I believe, certainly was the biggest and most sustained thrill that I ever had in broadcasting baseball.

I hope this serves your purpose.
Best regards,
Ronald Reagan

The Cubs have been immortalized in song, story, and poem ("Tinker-to-Evers-to-Chance"), and have been involved in some of the most memorable and fabled events in baseball history:

- Fred Merkle's "boner" in 1908
- Baseball's only "double no-hitter," between Jim "Hippo" Vaughn of the Cubs and Fred Toney of Cincinnati on May 2, 1917
- Babe Ruth's "called shot" off the Cubs' Charlie Root in Wrigley Field in the 1932 World Series
- Gabby Hartnett's "homer in the gloamin'" in 1938
- Pete Rose's 4,191st hit on September 8, 1985, that tied him with Ty Cobb for the most hits in baseball history
- Kerry Wood's record 20-strikeout game in 1998

Through their sometimes glorious, sometimes inept history, many of the game's greatest players have worn the uniform of the Cubs, but it is typical of their bad fortune—and no surprise to Cubs fans—that some of these players were Cubs before they attained stardom (Greg Maddux, Lou Brock, Dennis Eckersley, Rafael Palmeiro, Rube Waddell, Eddie Stanky) and others became Cubs in the twilight of great careers (Roger Bresnahan, Jimmie Foxx, Rogers Hornsby, Rabbit Maranville, Larry Bowa, Richie Ashburn, Ralph Kiner, Burleigh Grimes, Dizzy Dean, Tony Lazzeri, Fred Lindstrom, Robin Roberts, Hoyt Wilhelm, Monte Irvin).

Nevertheless, there is a plethora of stars who have spent all or most of their careers as Cubs, achieved stardom on Chicago's North Side, and are closely identified with the Cubs—players such as Hall of Famers Ernie "Mr. Cub"

Banks, Billy Williams, Gabby Hartnett, Mordecai "Three-Finger" Brown, Frank Chance, Joe Tinker, Johnny Evers, Billy Herman, Kiki Cuyler, Ferguson Jenkins, Hack Wilson, and newly elected Ryne Sandberg.

And there are others who await their call from Cooperstown—Bruce Sutter, Lee Smith, Ed Reulbach, Hippo Vaughn, Phil Cavarretta, Sammy Sosa, and Ronald Edward Santo, who is easily the greatest third baseman in Cubs history (nobody is close) and whose association with the Cubs began in 1960 and continues to this day as a broadcaster.

That gives Ron Santo an almost 50-year connection with the Cubs and makes him uniquely qualified to attempt the daunting task of selecting his all-time Cubs team—five players at each position plus the five best Cubs managers.

—Phil Pepe

Acknowledgments

The authors wish to acknowledge and thank the many people who helped in the preparation of this book, particularly those who so willingly and generously gave of their time to talk about Cubs past and present: "Mr. Cub," the incomparable Ernie Banks; Don Zimmer; Ralph Kiner; Ralph Branca; Bobby Thomson; Ryne Sandberg; Tom Seaver; Davey Lopes; Randy Hundley; Tommy John; Len Merullo; Rusty Staub; and Jim Kaat.

Our thanks, too, to the remarkable Ken Samelson, the wizard of statistics and little-known facts; to "the Dean," Jerome Holtzman, Chicago's, and the nation's, baseball historian; and to Moe Resner, whose devotion to the Cubs goes all the way back to the forties and extends all the way from Chicago to New Jersey.

Introduction

What a year 2005 has been for me! First I was informed that the Baseball Writers Association of America had elected me to the Baseball Hall of Fame, which is the ultimate honor and compliment any baseball player can receive. It's a humbling feeling to be included among the 200 or so greatest players who ever played the game of baseball, especially when I think about those that preceded me into the hallowed halls in Cooperstown, New York: Babe Ruth, Ty Cobb, Rogers Hornsby, Joe DiMaggio, Ted Williams, Mickey Mantle, Willie Mays, and Ernie Banks.

It's overwhelming!

Then I learned that Ron Santo has selected me as the No. 1 second baseman in Chicago Cubs history. What more can a ballplayer ask?

I am grateful for the honor, and flattered, particularly since it comes from Ron Santo, someone I admire as a man, respect as a player, and consider a close friend.

My one regret is that I never got to play alongside Ron (I arrived in Chicago in 1982, eight years after he retired), and I never got to see him play. But I have looked at the back of his baseball card and his numbers are tremendous—more than 2,200 hits, 342 home runs, over 1,300 runs batted in, and four seasons with more than 100 RBIs. And to think he did all that, playing 15 years in the major leagues, while battling diabetes throughout his career.

To play baseball and keep up with the lifestyle—the late hours, irregular eating and sleeping, night games, the travel, flying coast to coast at all hours—and to do it while taking insulin to control his diabetes, and to still put up the numbers he did is unbelievable. He was going against some very long odds, but he beat those odds and had a great career.

When I was traded to the Cubs, I got to know Ron because he was around a lot. He lived in Chicago and he stayed connected with the Cubs. Later, he got the job broadcasting Cubs games on the radio, and I saw him on a daily basis. We spent a lot of time talking baseball. I enjoyed being with him because of his knowledge of the game, his enthusiasm, and his passion for the Cubs. It's as if he lives and breathes Chicago Cubs baseball, which had a lot to do—in addition to his playing record—with the organization retiring his number.

Santo and I have a few other things in common besides being former Cubs. We're both from the state of Washington—I was born in Spokane, Ron in Seattle; we both have a home in Chicago—Ron lives there year-round, I have a home in downtown Chicago and we spend a lot of time there every year and get out to Wrigley Field often. And we both have a great, undying love for the Cubs.

It's hard to explain to people what's so special about being a Cub, or a Cubs fan. But it *is* special. It's Wrigley Field, so small and intimate that fans are close enough to the field to carry on conversations with the players. It's day baseball. It's the fact that Chicago is centrally located and the Cubs' fan base is stretched across the country.

Anybody who visits Chicago is told the one thing you must do is go to a game at Wrigley Field. So many people come through Chicago to go to school, to work, to visit, that they often get caught up in Cubs mania.

Cubs fans are unique. They're loyal and their love for the Cubs has been handed down from generation to generation, from grandfathers and grandmothers, to fathers and mothers, to sons and daughters. Some things haven't changed in 75 years. People have seats that have been in their family for decades.

Oh, yes, there's one more thing about being a Cubs fan: the anguish. It has been 60 years since the Cubs played in a World Series and almost 100 years since they won one, and Cubs fans are united in their despair . . . and in their hope every spring that this year will be their year.

That spirit does not exist only for the fans. It's also there with former Cubs, and the organization fosters it with the annual Cubs Convention that kicks off every new year. It's a great tradition that began in 1985, with old

Cubs getting together, including a few from the forties and many more from the fifties, sixties, seventies, and eighties. It was at these conventions that I got to meet and know former Cubs like Andy Pafko, Phil Cavarretta, Ernie Banks, Billy Williams, Glenn Beckert, Randy Hundley, Ferguson Jenkins, Rick Monday, and many others. We were from different eras, from different parts of the country, but we have one thing in common: we're all Cubs.

Earlier, I said that being elected to the Hall of Fame and being named by Ron Santo as the No. 1 second baseman in Cubs history has made 2005 a great year for me, and I asked, "What more can a ballplayer ask?"

Well, there is one more thing. As I write this, I am awaiting word from the Veterans Committee on their selections for the Hall of Fame. Among those under consideration is Ron Santo, and if the members of the Committee take a close look at his statistics, I feel they have no choice but to vote him in.

Wouldn't that be something? Santo and I being inducted at the same time? Cooperstown would turn into Chicago East. I don't know if that little hamlet in New York State can handle that.

I don't want to appear greedy here, but while I'm wishing for things, I have just one more request. The Cubs in the 2005 World Series. Not just in it—winning it.

Wouldn't that be something?

—Ryne Sandberg

FEW AND CHOSEN

ONE

Catcher

BEFORE ERNIE BANKS, the shining light of Chicago Cubs baseball was **Charles Leo Hartnett**, who picked up the ironic nickname "Gabby" because as a Cubs rookie in 1922, he was shy and reticent in the presence of such hardened veterans as Charlie Hollocher, Bob O'Farrell, and Grover Cleveland Alexander.

Gabby was the oldest of 14 children in an athletic family. His father was a streetcar conductor and a semipro catcher who was a legend in New England because of an exceptional throwing arm. Three Hartnett sisters barnstormed with a women's team, and three brothers played semipro ball, but Gabby was the only one to make it to the major leagues. He replaced O'Farrell as the Cubs' regular catcher in 1924 and held down that post until 1940, when in his third season as manager of the Cubs, he turned the catching chores over to veteran Al Todd, acquired in a trade with the Dodgers.

1. CHARLES LEO "GABBY" HARTNETT

2. RANDY HUNDLEY

3. JODY DAVIS

4. JOHNNY KLING

5. BOB SCHEFFING

In a 20-year career, Hartnett caught 100 or more games 12 times, led the National League in putouts 4 times, led in assists and fielding percentage 6

The 1935 National League Most Valuable Player, Hartnett was considered by many to be the best catcher of his era. *Photo courtesy of AP/Wide World Photos.*

times, had a career batting average of .297, belted 236 home runs, and drove in 1,179 runs.

Until Roy Campanella, Yogi Berra, Johnny Bench, and Carlton Fisk came along, the debate over who was the greatest catcher in baseball history always centered on three names: Mickey Cochrane of the Detroit Tigers and Bill Dickey of the New York Yankees in the American League, and Hartnett in the National League. Joe McCarthy, who managed both Dickey and Hartnett and against Cochrane, called Hartnett "the perfect catcher."

Hartnett made the All-Star team six times and was the starting catcher for the National League three times, including the 1934 game at New York's Polo Grounds when he was behind the plate as Carl Hubbell struck out, in succession, future Hall of Famers Babe Ruth, Lou Gehrig, Jimmie Foxx, Al Simmons, and Joe Cronin.

In 1935, Hartnett was named the National League's Most Valuable Player when he batted .344, third in the league, and had 13 home runs and 91 RBIs. But his most productive season came five years earlier, when there was no MVP selected. In 1930, Hartnett batted .339, had 37 home runs (a record for a catcher that stood until Campanella slugged 41 23 years later), and drove in 122 runs.

I regret I never got to meet Hartnett, but I have heard so much about him from old-time Cubs fans and former players that I feel as if I knew him. They say he was the best at his position, a great defensive catcher, and, of course, there was the famous home run. You can't live in Chicago as long as I have and not have heard a lot about the great Gabby Hartnett.

But he was overshadowed by the Giants' Bill Terry, the last National Leaguer to bat over .400, and by Hartnett's Cubs teammate Hack Wilson, who led the league with 56 home runs and a record 191 runs batted in.

Hartnett's greatest moment in baseball is one that is revered by Cubs fans to this day, almost seven decades after it happened. Hartnett, 37 years old and on the downside of his career, had replaced Charlie Grimm as manager of the Cubs in the middle of the 1938 season with the team in third place. On September 28, the Cubs met the first-place Pirates in Wrigley Field with Pittsburgh holding a half-game lead on Chicago. With darkness falling rapidly (remember, there were no lights in Wrigley Field) and the score tied, 5–5, in the ninth, Hartnett came to bat with two outs and nobody on base. The count went to 0–2 when Hartnett blasted his famous "homer in the gloamin'" to give the Cubs a 6–5 victory. With the victory, the Cubs moved into first place to stay, and they finished two games ahead of the Pirates to win the National League pennant.

When the Cubs slipped to fourth place in 1939 and fifth in 1940, Hartnett was fired as manager and replaced by Jimmie Wilson. Gabby would play a final season with the Giants in 1941, batting .300 in 64 games at age 40.

In 1955, Hartnett was elected to the Baseball Hall of Fame, joining Ray Schalk of the White Sox as the seventh and eighth catchers so honored (six other catchers have since been inducted). A native of Woonsocket, Rhode Island, Hartnett is one of only three natives of the smallest state in the union to be elected to the Hall of Fame. The others are Napoleon Lajoie, also a

3

native of Woonsocket, and Hugh Duffy of Cranston, another former Cub, who both started their careers before 1900.

I regret I never got to meet Hartnett, but I have heard so much about him from old-time Cubs fans and former players that I feel as if I knew him. They say he was the best at his position, a great defensive catcher, and, of course, there was the famous home run. You can't live in Chicago as long as I have and not have heard a lot about the great Gabby Hartnett.

My old teammate Randy Hundley told me he once met Hartnett at a banquet and had a nice conversation with him—the two best catchers in Cubs history side by side on the dais. Hundley said he noticed a big ring on Hartnett's finger and Randy asked him, "Is that a World Series ring?"

"No, son," Hartnett replied. "That's a Hall of Fame ring."

Randy said he was so embarrassed, he wanted to crawl under the table.

•

Speaking of **Randy Hundley**, the best compliment I can pay my old buddy is that he's a guy you would want with you in a foxhole. "Rebel"—that's what we called him because he's from Virginia and has a deep voice and a Southern drawl—is a born-again Christian. He doesn't drink, and he doesn't smoke, and he never cussed. Never. But he didn't wear his beliefs on his sleeve, and he could get mad. He was a guy who would not turn the other cheek.

Rebel was tough and aggressive. Very aggressive. He'd sit behind the plate and pop his fist into his mitt right in a hitter's ear. We had a brawl with Pittsburgh one day, and my roommate, Glenn Beckert, was in the middle of it. I went in there and tried to pull him out, and I saw this body go over me. It was Hundley. He had jumped right into the middle of the melee—literally flew over me to grab a Pirate.

The Cubs have been criticized over the years for some of the bad trades they made, like Lou Brock for Ernie Broglio, but they made some good trades, too, and one of the best was when they sent Lindy McDaniel, Don Landrum, and Jim Rittwage to the Giants after the 1965 season for two young, unproven players: pitcher Bill Hands and Hundley. That trade helped the Cubs work their way to becoming contenders over the next seven years.

Hands won 54 games in the three-year period from 1968 through 1970, and Hundley became the Cubs' best catcher since Gabby Hartnett. He was a great receiver, had a good arm, and was an iron man behind the plate. He set

My old buddy "Rebel" was one of those players I'd want in my foxhole. Here he's shown conferring with Cardinals manager Red Schoendienst and Mets pitcher Jerry Koosman during the 1969 All-Star Game in Washington. *Photo courtesy of Focus on Sport/Getty Images.*

one major league record by catching in 160 games in 1968, and another by catching in 150 games or more for three consecutive seasons, 1967–69.

Hundley won the Gold Glove in 1967 when he committed only four errors all season, a National League record. He also was the first one-handed catcher. He developed a catcher's mitt that was a lot like a first baseman's, loose and flexible. It allowed him to catch with one hand and keep his throwing hand behind his back to avoid getting hit on his right hand by foul tips. A lot of catchers catch that way now, but Rebel was the first.

And Hundley was a much better hitter than people give him credit for. When he was young, he could run, and he had power. In that ill-fated 1969 season, he was a key guy in our lineup. He batted .255, hit 18 home runs, and drove in 67 runs, so he was a guy opposing pitchers had to respect.

A baseball lifer, Don Zimmer has done it all in almost 60 years in the game—player, coach, minor league manager, major league manager. His connection with the Cubs began in 1960 when the Dodgers sent him to Chicago in a trade. Later, he served as a Cubs coach under his childhood friend from Cincinnati, manager Jim Frey. When Frey took over as general manager of the Cubs in 1988, he brought Zim back to manage the team. Zimmer guided the Cubs to the National League East title in 1989. And they didn't win anything again until they captured the NL Central in 2003.

"When I took over the club," said Zimmer, "I figured one position that was set was catcher. We had Jody Davis, and he was a big, strong kid. I had seen him have his best years when I was a third-base coach. He was one of the Cubs' big players in the eighties. He could catch, and he could throw, and he had power. A good player, and a fan favorite.

"When I managed the Red Sox, the fans in Boston would chant whenever Luis Tiant was pitching: 'Loo-ey . . . Loo-ey . . .' In Chicago, they did the same thing when Davis came to bat: 'Jo-dy . . . Jo-dy . . .' They loved him, and he had some big years for the Cubs."

Davis had been the Cubs' best hitter when they lost to the Padres in the 1984 National League Championship Series, batting .389 with two home runs and six RBIs. The year before Zimmer took over as manager, Davis had batted .248 with 19 homers and 51 RBIs—a drop-off from previous years but still good enough to hold his job as the Cubs' No. 1 catcher.

"I realized he was on the downside," said Zimmer, "but I still thought he had enough left. I wanted Jody Davis to be my catcher, but he started to slip, and when I played Damon Berryhill, he produced more than Davis, so I had no choice but to use Berryhill more and more."

In 1988, Zimmer's first year as Cubs manager, Davis played in only 88 games and batted .229, with six homers and 33 RBIs. It was clear he was at the end of the line, so late in the season, the Cubs traded him to Atlanta for a couple of pitchers.

"I never saw the best of Jody Davis as a manager," said Zimmer, "but I saw the best of him when I was a coach. He was an outstanding catcher: a good hitter, a fan favorite, a great guy, and a great family man."

Unfortunately, Rebel began to wear down after the 1969 season from catching all those games. Then he hurt both his knees, and he never was the same again. But he had the great pleasure of watching his son, Todd, set a major league record for catchers (since broken) when he hit 41 home runs for the Mets in 1996.

Today, Randy operates the Cubs' Fantasy Camp in Arizona, and many of us from the 1969 team get together in January to reminisce about the good old days, tell stories, and have a ball.

Jody Davis was an outstanding defensive catcher. A thinking man's catcher, an excellent receiver with a great arm, and a leader. Jody was a lot like Hundley in his demeanor. And he was a good hitter. In a five-year period with the Cubs, from 1983 to 1987, he hit exactly 100 homers and drove in 361 runs. Twice he hit more than 20 homers, and his 94 RBIs in 1984 is second to Gabby Hartnett's 122 in 1930 for the most by a Cubs catcher.

In the 1984 NLCS against the Padres, Jody came up big, batting .389 with two homers and six RBIs, and he hit a huge home run in the fifth game of that series. At least it was huge at the time. It came in the second inning, and it gave the Cubs a 3–0 lead. Unfortunately, the Padres came back to score six runs and win the game, 6–3, and once again the Cubs were denied a chance to go to the World Series.

Catching is such a tough job, such a physical grind, there have been very few in the history of baseball who produced big offensive numbers, and the rigors of catching took their toll on Davis.

Jody was traded to Atlanta late in the 1988 season and finished out his career with the Braves, but he never came close to putting up the numbers for the Braves that he did for the Cubs in that five-year stretch.

The great Cubs teams in the early 1900s had so many stars, it was easy for an excellent player to be overlooked and that, apparently, is what happened to **Johnny Kling**, who was Chicago's catcher from 1900 to 1911.

Although a fair hitter—he batted .272 for 13 big-league seasons—Kling was known mostly for his defense and was considered the premier defensive catcher of his day. Ed Reulbach, who won 181 major league games, called him "one of the greatest catchers who ever wore a mask."

Davis, here with Rick Sutcliffe at the center of the team's celebration after clinching the 1984 NL Eastern Division, was a huge contributor that season with 94 RBIs—second only to Hartnett (122) for RBIs in a season by a Cubs catcher. *Photo courtesy of Bettmann/CORBIS.*

Kling led the National League catchers in fielding four times, in putouts six times, in assists twice, and in double plays once. In one game in 1907, he threw out all four Cardinals runners who attempted to steal second, and in the World Series that year, he held Ty Cobb, at the time baseball's greatest running threat, without a stolen base.

As good a catcher as he was, Kling was more talented in another area. He was a world-champion pocket billiards player and quit baseball in 1909 to concentrate on billiards. When he was defeated in his attempt to retain his world billiards title, he returned to the Cubs in 1910 but could not regain his starting position from his replacement, Jimmy Archer.

Like Kling, Archer was an outstanding defensive catcher with a powerful arm and was regarded as the best-throwing catcher of his time, which merits his inclusion among the list of greatest catchers in Cubs' history.

Bob Scheffing was my first manager, although I never played for him. He was managing the Cubs in my first spring training in 1959. I was sent to Double A San Antonio that first year, and when I got to the Cubs the next year, Scheffing had been replaced as manager.

9

Kling, behind the plate during a game in 1909, was considered the premier defensive catcher of his day. *Photo courtesy of the Rucker Archive.*

Scheffing, shown here diving to thwart a steal attempt by Brooklyn's Jackie Robinson, earned considerable renown for his defensive abilities. *Photo courtesy of AP/Wide World Photos.*

Although he was a fine defensive catcher and a .300 hitter with the Cubs in 1948, Scheffing is known more for what he accomplished after his playing career than for what he did during it. After he was let go by the Cubs, he managed the Detroit Tigers, and his 1961 Tigers won 101 games but finished second to the Yankees in the American League. Two years later, he was fired by the Tigers and moved upstairs into the broadcast booth alongside the great Ernie Harwell. Later, Scheffing became general manager of the Mets, and his 1973 Mets team, with Yogi Berra as manager, won the National League pennant.

They don't make my list; nevertheless, I want to make mention of two others who caught for Chicago in the early days. One is Roger Bresnahan, the second catcher elected to the Baseball Hall of Fame. But, typical of Cubs' bad timing, he was in Chicago only before and after his Hall of Fame years.

The other is someone I know nothing about because he played before 1900, but how could I completely ignore a guy with a name like Silver Flint?

Statistical Summaries

All statistics are for player's Cubs career only.

HITTING

G = Games

H = Hits

HR = Home runs

RBI = Runs batted in

SB = Stolen bases

BA = Batting average

Catcher	Years	G	H	HR	RBI	SB	BA
Gabby Hartnett *First catcher to hit more than 200 home runs*	1922–40	1,926	1,867	231	1,153	28	.297
Randy Hundley *Last NL catcher to win a Gold Glove before Johnny Bench won 10 straight from 1968 to 1977*	1966–73 1976–77	947	758	80	364	12	.240

continued	Years	G	H	HR	RBI	SB	BA
Jody Davis *Led NL catchers in putouts, assists, and double plays in 1986*	1981–88	990	834	122	467	7	.251
Johnny Kling *Twice stole 23 bases in a season (1902, 1903)*	1900–08 1910–11	1,024	960	16	436	118	.271
Bob Scheffing *Slugged pinch-hit grand slam on September 20, 1941, against Cardinals*	1941–42 1946–50	437	311	16	165	6	.266

FIELDING

PO = Putouts

A = Assists

E = Errors

DP = Double plays

TC/G = Total chances divided by games played

FA = Fielding average

Catcher	PO	A	E	DP	TC/G	FA
Gabby Hartnett	1,759	1,239	138	162	4.8	.984
Randy Hundley	5,346	447	47	59	6.2	.992
Jody Davis	5,124	597	75	64	6.0	.987
Johnny Kling	4,585	1,244	161	97	6.2	.973
Bob Scheffing	1,219	149	23	23	4.3	.983

TWO

First Baseman

H<small>E'S "M<small>R</small>. C<small>UB</small>," AND DESERVEDLY SO</small>: the most popular player in the team's 100-plus-year history. Nobody else is even close. He's No. 1. There is no No. 2.

Ernie Banks is "Mr. Cub" for the 512 home runs he hit, the 1,636 runs he batted in, the 11 All-Star selections, the two MVPs (in consecutive seasons, 1958 and 1959), the two home-run championships, the two RBI championships, the 19 major league seasons, the 2,528 games he played—every one of them in a Cubs uniform—and his election to the Hall of Fame. And more. Much, much more.

He's "Mr. Cub" for his warmth, his loyalty, his sunny disposition, and his perpetual smile. He's "Mr. Cub" because

1. E<small>RNIE</small> B<small>ANKS</small>

2. C<small>AP</small> A<small>NSON</small>

3. P<small>HIL</small> C<small>AVARRETTA</small>

4. M<small>ARK</small> G<small>RACE</small>

5. B<small>ILL</small> B<small>UCKNER</small>

he has never forgotten his roots; because he is a one-man advertisement for Wrigley Field, day baseball, and the city of Chicago; and because he makes you feel good just being around him.

I have known Ernie Banks for more than 45 years, and he is the same person today as he was on June 26, 1960, when I joined the Cubs as a frightened-to-death

Banks, the ever-popular "Mr. Cub," dug a lot of my throws out of the dirt after he moved to first base later in his career. *Photo courtesy of AP/Wide World Photos.*

14

20-year-old rookie. I was sitting in the dugout, and Ernie came out and sat next to me and said, "You nervous, kid?" I said, "Gosh, yeah."

I have known Ernie for more than 45 years, and in all that time, I have never heard him say a bad word about anybody (or anything), and I have never heard anybody say a bad word about him.

People who meet him for the first time, who hear him expound for the first time on the beauty of baseball, the Cubs, Wrigley Field, and life in general, think it's all an act, a façade. They keep waiting for him to drop his guard, but he never does. I have known him for more than 45 years and I, too, have waited for him to drop his guard, to be anything but upbeat, positive, and optimistic. I'm still waiting.

With Ernie, what you see and what you hear is what you get. His enthusiasm, his optimism, his goodness—I can honestly say it's all genuine.

You would think, somewhere along the line, you would get up in the morning and come to the ballpark and maybe things aren't going well, you're not going to be in a good mood. Not Ernie. If anything was bothering him, you would never know with Ernie Banks. Never! If it was raining, he'd walk in and say, "Hey, let's play two today." It's pouring down rain and we'd all say, "Oh, Ernie."

I played my whole career with him and saw him almost every day. He was always the same cheery guy.

Our lockers were near each other's. It was Ernie, then Billy Williams, and then me, all in a row. If Ernie hit a home run to win a ballgame, or hit two home runs in a game, the Chicago writers and the visiting writers would all come in and crowd around his locker for a story, and the first thing he would say, every time, was, "Do you guys know Billy Williams and Ron Santo?"

What a hitter he was! Ernie Banks had a beautiful swing, and some of his home runs were simply majestic. He could hit the ball onto Waveland Avenue, but most of his home runs were these vicious line drives that would get out of there in a blink of an eye. He wasn't very big, just 6'1" and 180 pounds, but he had lightning-fast hands and powerful wrists.

The writers would ask their questions—"Did you hit a fastball?"—and Ernie would just smile at them and say, "Ohh, I don't know what I hit."

That's Ernie. We'd go out to dinner and he was the same bubbly guy in public that he was in the clubhouse. He was funny to be around. A good sense of humor. Talking all the time. People would come up to him, and he would talk to all of them. He'd never blow anybody off. I'm convinced that if he had run for mayor of Chicago, he would have won in a landslide.

Ernie was a great teammate, and he's a great guy. He's still one of my dearest friends. Ernie is a guy who has never forgotten where he came from, and I think that's so important in life. I don't care how successful you are, you have to remember how you got there. Ernie has.

He was born and raised in Dallas, and he was a high school star in basketball, football, and track. He preferred softball to baseball, but when he was 17, he signed to play with a Negro barnstorming baseball team for the money, $15 a game. The Kansas City Monarchs spotted him and signed him to a contract, but he soon left the Monarchs to spend two years in military service. After the army hitch, Ernie returned to the Monarchs, where the Cubs scouted him and offered him a contract.

Banks went right to the Cubs and became their regular shortstop (I'll talk more about that later in the chapter on shortstops) without ever playing a game in the minor leagues, and he was their first African-American player, which had to be difficult for him back in 1953. Knowing Ernie, his sunny disposition helped him get through the rough times and won over his teammates. His booming bat didn't hurt, either. In his first full season, 1954, he hit 19 home runs. The next year, he belted 44, then the most ever for a shortstop.

By the time I got to Chicago in 1960, Ernie was a full-fledged star and one of the best power hitters in the game. From 1955 through 1960, he hit more home runs than any other major leaguer, and that included Henry Aaron, Willie Mays, and Mickey Mantle.

What a hitter he was! He had a beautiful swing, and some of his home runs were simply majestic. He could hit the ball onto Waveland Avenue, but most of his home runs were these vicious line drives that would get out of there in a blink of an eye. He wasn't very big, just 6'1" and 180 pounds, but he had lightning-fast hands and powerful wrists.

My first two years with the Cubs, Ernie was still playing shortstop and I was playing right alongside him. In 1962, he moved to first base and, let me tell you, throwing to him, you could close your eyes and you knew he would come up with the ball. He had such soft hands; he dug a lot of balls out of the dirt. Those soft hands saved me quite a few errors.

This will give you an idea of what kind of man Ernie Banks is. After the 1959 season, the Cubs wanted to have a day in his honor. Ernie modestly declined, saying he hadn't been around long enough to be worthy of such an honor. He finally relented and had his day five years later.

When he retired after the 1971 season, the Cubs had a flag made up with Ernie's No. 14 on it and raised it on the left-field foul pole. Fittingly, his uniform number was the first one ever retired by the Cubs.

If there's one regret about Banks' career, it's that he is one of very few Hall of Famers who never played in the postseason. That's one reason losing the pennant in 1969 was such a blow to us. Sure, we wanted to win it for ourselves. But most of us wanted to win it for Ernie even more.

Chicago baseball historians tell me that no all-time Cubs team would be complete if it didn't include **Cap Anson**. I'll just have to take their word for it. I don't know much about this man Adrian Constantine Anson, called "Pop," or "Cap," who played his last game 43 years before I was born and died 18 years before I was born, except for what I have heard and read about him. And everything I have heard and read makes him out to be one of the great stars of baseball of the dim, distant past, before 1900.

What I have learned is that old Cap was not only a great player but also a great leader of men, and he deserves a place on my all-time Cubs team as both a first baseman and a manager. I'll hold off talking about his leadership skills and cover that in the chapter on managers and deal here only with Cap Anson, the player, all of my knowledge obtained from the mouths of others or from lines in a record book.

A good place to start is with his lifetime batting average: .329 in 22 seasons, all with the Chicago team in the National League, from 1876 to 1897 (his career actually predates the National League with five seasons in the National Association, 27 years in all at the highest level of baseball competition), before they were called "Cubs." He was the first player to reach 3,000 hits, and he won three batting championships, one with an average of .399 in 1881.

Anson's playing career actually spanned 27 years, and he was the first player in history to reach 3,000 hits. *Photo courtesy of MLB Photos/Getty Images.*

*R*alph Kiner, a Hall of Fame slugger and the premier home-run hitter of his era, had a professional relationship with Phil Cavarretta on three levels. The Cubs' first baseman was Kiner's opponent, his teammate, and his manager.

Cavarretta was one year past winning the National League's Most Valuable Player Award when Kiner broke in with the Pittsburgh Pirates in 1946. Kiner led the National League in home runs with 23 as a 23-year-old rookie, while Cavarretta, at age 31, batted a respectable .296 for the Cubs.

"Cavarretta was a terrific left-handed batter," Kiner remembered. "He came out of Lane Tech High School in Chicago, a very good high school with a great baseball team, and Cavarretta went right from high school to the major leagues at the age of 17. He never played in the minor leagues. That proves he really was a good hitter to be able to do that in those days. Cavarretta was a line-drive-type hitter with good power to the alleys, not a home-run hitter, but a guy who hit a lot of doubles [182 of them in a six-year period, from 1942 through 1947].

"Cavarretta was an unusual hitter," said Kiner. "He was in the style of the Charlie Lau and Walt Hrniak school of hitting, with the top hand off the bat. He would slap the ball around the ballpark to all fields. He wasn't typical of the first basemen of his day. He was small for a first baseman, and he didn't hit home runs, but he was a good hitter, and a good all-around ballplayer."

In 1947, as Cavarretta's career was beginning to wind down, Kiner and Johnny Mize tied for the National League lead in home runs with 51 and became the fifth and sixth players in baseball history to hit at least 50 homers for a season (Babe Ruth four times, Jimmie Foxx twice, Hank Greenberg, Hack Wilson, Mize, and Kiner).

Kiner led the league or tied for the league lead in home runs in each of his first seven seasons, accumulating 294 in that stretch for an average of 42 homers per year.

Bothered by a bad back, Kiner had hit only seven home runs in 41 games when the Pirates traded him with Joe Garagiola, George Metkovich, and Howard Pollett to the Cubs for six players and $150,000 on June 4, 1953. Teamed with Hank Sauer to give the Cubs a potent one-two home-run punch, Kiner's home-run bat awakened in the second half of the season as he blasted 28 out of the park in 117 games. It was in those 117 games that Kiner got to know Cavarretta up close and personal, as his teammate and his manager.

"He didn't have much success as a manager," said Kiner, "and he was the only manager that ever got fired during spring training. I remember it well because I was on the team with the Cubs at the time. It was 1954. Phil Wrigley was the owner of the ballclub at the time, and Phil Wrigley never came to the ballpark. He never saw a game at Wrigley Field. He watched all the games on television when they were televising them, but he never showed up at the ballpark.

"Wrigley had an open-door policy in his office in the Wrigley Building in downtown Chicago. Anybody could walk into his office at any time and talk to him. He was very pleasant and nice to talk to. Before the season, Wrigley called Cavarretta to his office, and he made the mistake of asking Cavarretta where he thought the Cubs would finish that year. Maybe it was Cavarretta who made the mistake of answering. He said, 'This team is going to finish last.' This was before the season started, and that wasn't what Wrigley wanted to hear. He didn't like that negative approach, so Wrigley fired Phil in spring training and gave the job to Stan Hack.

"There are two people I have known in baseball who had what you would call dual personalities," said Kiner. "One was Eddie Stanky, and the other was Phil Cavarretta. They were the most pleasant people off the field, but on the field they were impossible to get along with. Once they put on that uniform, their whole personality changed. Phil was a great competitor, and he took losses as hard as anyone I ever saw. As a manager, he really was a Dr. Jekyll and Mr. Hyde."

Apparently, Anson was no fancy Dan with the glove. He started out as a catcher and third baseman, but when he took over the White Stockings, he exercised a manager's prerogative and put himself permanently at first base, where he apparently was a defensive liability. But who could argue with the boss?

He holds the career record for errors by a first baseman, 657, a staggering total until you realize that in those days, fielders did not use gloves. Just the thought of Mark Grace having to catch throws from Shawon Dunston bare-handed makes me wince in pain.

Anson also led the league in RBIs eight times and once hit 21 home runs in a season, 1884, when home runs were rare. Even with the impressive total of 21, Anson was fourth in the league. The three players ahead of him were his teammates, Ned Williamson with 27, Fred Pfeffer with 25, and Abner Dalrymple with 22. Get this. The book tells me Chicago hit 142 home runs as a team that year, and no other team in the National League hit more than 39. There is an explanation, however. The Cubs (White Stockings) played their home games that season in Lake Front Park, where the left-field foul line measured 196 feet and the right-field line 180 feet. Talk about being born too late!

Here's another thing I learned about Cap Anson, which tells us a lot about the game in his day. In 9,108 at-bats, he struck out only 294 times, or one strikeout for every 31 at-bats.

Phil Cavarretta was a baseball owner's dream: a local boy, born and raised in Chicago, who played for the home team; the son of Italian immigrants in a city with a large Italian-American population; a blue-collar worker who punched the clock every day, played in at least 125 games for six straight seasons in the forties, and held down first base for the Cubs for two decades.

I'm impressed that the man played in the big leagues at the age of 17, and at how good he was. He was amazing. A four-time All-Star, a batting champion, a Most Valuable Player, an excellent first baseman, and a vital member of the Cubs' last National League championship team.

Philip Joseph Cavarretta was born on July 19, 1916, attended Chicago's Lane Tech, and signed a contract with Peoria of the Central League before he had graduated from high school. He joined the Cubs on September 16, 1934, two months after his 18th birthday, and became the regular first baseman for the National League champion Cubs in 1935 at the age of 19. Cavarretta was a Cub for 20 consecutive seasons—the longest tenure in team history—including two and a half seasons as a player/manager. He ended his career, regrettably, by playing his final 77 games with the Cubs' South Side rivals, the Chicago White Sox. (Who am I to talk? I also ended my career with the White Sox.)

Cavarretta was not the prototypical big, burly, slow-footed, slugging first baseman of his day. He stood only 5'11", weighed 175 pounds, and never hit more than 10 home runs in any season (only 95 in 2,030 major league games). But he was a fancy-Dan fielder around the bag, and a slashing line-drive hitter often compared with his contemporary, the Cardinals' Stan Musial, the National League's premier hitter of his time. Cavarretta had 1,977 hits and struck out only 598 times in 6,754 major league at-bats, and he was the perfect No. 2 or No. 3 batter in front of Cubs sluggers Chuck Klein, Ripper Collins, Bill Nicholson, and Andy Pafko.

Exempt from military service because of an ear ailment, Cavarretta had his greatest years during World War II. He tied Musial for the league lead in hits with 197 in 1944, and in that season's All-Star Game in Pittsburgh, he reached base five times. The following year he led the National League in batting with a .355 average, the highest in Cubs history for a left-handed hitter; was named the league's Most Valuable Player; and batted .423 in the World Series, won by the Detroit Tigers, four games to three.

Cavarretta, shown here stretching to retire Detroit's Mickey Cochrane during the 1935 World Series at Wrigley Field, is still among the Cubs' all-time leaders in several categories. *Photo courtesy of Bettmann/CORBIS.*

When his playing career was over, Cavarretta managed in the minor leagues, coached and scouted in the Tigers organization, and was a greatly respected hitting instructor for the expansion New York Mets.

To this day, more than a half century after his playing career, Phil Cavarretta's name appears among the Cubs' all-time top 10 in games played, at-bats, runs,

Grace was a real throwback to my era and before, when ballplayers played with passion, aggressiveness, and a real love for the game. *Photo courtesy of AP/Wide World Photos.*

hits, singles, triples, extra-base hits, RBIs, and walks, and people in Chicago still talk about him and how great a player he was.

Until the past few years, Cavarretta used to come to Wrigley Field quite often, and I got to know him. What a wonderful man! Two things about him stood out for me, in addition to his outstanding record. One was that he was such a little guy, especially for a first baseman. The other was that he obviously loved the game and loved to talk baseball, and I enjoyed talking with him. Every time I'd see him, we would talk about baseball, and you could tell how much he respected the game. I love that. You just don't see that very much with today's players.

Mark Grace is a guy who could have played with me, and that's high praise coming from this old timer. Like most guys who played in my era, the sixties and seventies, I like to think we played the game right: with passion and aggressiveness, and with a love and respect for the game.

Mark is one of those guys. He was old school. He loved the game of baseball. He was a good team man and a great defensive first baseman. He won four Gold Gloves, but he should have won more. By that I mean he deserved to win more, that's how good he was at first base. He was one of the best-fielding first basemen I ever saw. And a great, great hitter. He could flat-out hit. He understood hitting. He had 2,445 hits for his career and the most hits of anybody during the decade of the nineties. And he had 1,146 career RBIs.

The only thing he didn't do well was hit home runs—only 173 in his career, never more than 17 in any one season. But he was outstanding in every other department.

The man had 2,715 hits. He drove in 1,208 runs for a singles hitter. Think about it! He played 22 seasons. And he had a lifetime batting average of .289. Look at his numbers. Those are Hall of Fame numbers, or close to it, but **Bill Buckner** will be remembered for one thing: the ball he let go through his legs that cost the Boston Red Sox the 1986 World Series. And that's a shame.

It's a shame because Buckner had such a great career and did so many good things, and because he's such a good guy. Billy Buck is a native Californian, but that incident in 1986 pretty much ran him out of California. He lives in Idaho now. He's laid back. He's a beautiful person. How can you look at one play to

In his 8 seasons with the Cubs, and his 14 additional seasons in the big leagues, Buckner was as hard-nosed a player as there was and never afraid to get his uniform dirty. *Photo courtesy of Getty Images.*

define a career? Sure, the timing wasn't good, but it could have happened to anybody. It just happened to him.

The only thing Buckner didn't do was hit home runs—174 in 22 seasons with a high of 18 for the Red Sox in that infamous season of 1986. Buckner, to me, is a lot like Mark Grace. Almost identical. I'd say Grace was a better fielder, but offensively they're very similar.

In fact, if you look at Phil Cavarretta, Mark Grace, and Bill Buckner, you can see a lot of similarities. All three were outstanding left-handed hitters. None of them put up big home-run numbers. You can throw a blanket over them when it comes to rating them as Cubs first basemen.

Then why did I pick them in the order of Cavarretta, Grace, Buckner?

Simply because Cavarretta played 20 years as a Cub, Grace 13 years, and Buckner 8.

Statistical Summaries

All statistics are for player's Cubs career only.

HITTING

G = Games

H = Hits

HR = Home runs

RBI = Runs batted in

SB = Stolen bases

BA = Batting average

First Baseman	Years	G	H	HR	RBI	SB	BA
Ernie Banks *Made only four errors in 153 games at first base in 1969*	1953–71	2,528	2,583	512	1,636	50	.274
Cap Anson *Scored record six runs in a game on August 24, 1886*	1876–97	2,276	2,995	97	1,879	247	.329
Phil Cavarretta *Hit over .400 in both 1938 and 1945 World Series*	1934–55	2,030	1,977	95	920	65	.293

continued	Years	G	H	HR	RBI	SB	BA
Mark Grace *Went 11 for 17 (.647) with eight RBIs in 1989 NL Championship Series vs. Giants*	1988–2000	1,910	2,201	148	1,004	67	.308
Bill Buckner *Had seven RBIs in 23–22 loss to Phillies on May 17, 1979*	1977–84	974	1,136	81	516	56	.300

FIELDING

PO = Putouts

A = Assists

E = Errors

DP = Double plays

TC/G = Total chances divided by games played

FA = Fielding average

First Baseman	PO	A	E	DP	TC/G	FA
Ernie Banks	12,005	809	80	1,005	10.2	.994
Cap Anson	20,794	955	583	1,189	10.9	.974
Phil Cavarretta	11,375	796	123	1,012	9.8	.990
Mark Grace	16,601	1,550	96	1,352	9.7	.995
Bill Buckner	8,100	744	71	663	10.4	.992

THREE

Second Baseman

NOBODY MADE PLAYING SECOND BASE LOOK EASIER than **Ryne Sandberg**. People used to criticize him because they said he would never dive for a ball. He never left his feet. Well, he didn't have to dive for a ball. That's how good he was. You don't compile fielding records like he did if you have to dive for balls.

Ryno was a shortstop in the minor leagues with the Phillies, but when the Cubs got him, they played him at third base the first year, then moved him to second base. In his first season as a second baseman, he won the Gold Glove, and then he won it for the next eight years. His career fielding percentage was .989. He made only 120 errors in more than ten thousand chances. In 1986, he set National League records for the fewest errors, five, and the highest fielding percentage, .9938, by a second baseman. And over the 1989–90 seasons, he set a major league record by playing 123 consecutive errorless games.

1. RYNE SANDBERG

2. BILLY HERMAN

3. GLENN BECKERT

4. JOHNNY EVERS

5. ROGERS HORNSBY

Talk about a great trade! This was probably the greatest one the Cubs ever made. It came on January 27, 1982. The Phillies were looking for a

The 1982 deal that landed then-22-year-old infielder Sandberg from the Phillies organization might go down as the greatest in Cubs history. *Photo courtesy of AP/Wide World Photos.*

proven major leaguer to take over as their regular shortstop, and the Cubs were looking for a veteran, stopgap shortstop. So they made a swap. The Cubs sent Ivan DeJesus, a proven veteran just 29 years old, to Philly, and the Phillies sent Larry Bowa, 36 years old and near the end of his career, to Chicago.

Our general manager at the time was Dallas Green, who had spent a lot of years in the Phillies' organization and knew all the players in their system very well. Dallas asked that Sandberg, who was just 22 at the time, be included in the deal, and the Phillies agreed.

It became a running gag for Bowa for years when he came into Chicago. He'd say to Ryno, "Don't forget, you were just a throw-in."

Some throw-in!

Sandberg was a Cub for 16 seasons and had a lifetime average of .285, 2,386 hits, 282 home runs, and 1,061 RBIs. He was a 10-time All-Star, hit 20 or more home runs in a season six times, led the league in homers with 40 in 1990, and led in triples with 19 in 1984 when he was the National League Most Valuable Player. And he had 344 steals with 20 or more in nine different seasons, including a high of 54 steals in 1985. He had that rare combination of power and speed, plus that great defense.

In that MVP year, Ryno needed one more triple and one more homer to be the first major leaguer with 200 hits and 20 doubles, triples, home runs, and stolen bases in the same season. The following year he was the third player in major league history to hit at least 25 homers and steal at least 50 bases in the same year.

Those accomplishments were hard to ignore, and I'm proud to say that the Baseball Writers of America recognized them and elected Ryno to the Hall of Fame in his third year of eligibility.

I never saw **Billy Herman** play, but I met him a couple of times when I was a young player and he came to old timers' games, and I heard a lot about him, especially from Leo Durocher. Leo used to say that Herman was the perfect No. 2 hitter: a master at hitting behind the runner.

Just look at his numbers. He had a lifetime batting average of .304. Eight times in his 15-year career, Herman batted over .300. In 1935, he led the National League in hits with 227 and doubles with 57, batted .341, and scored 113 runs. In 1939, he led the league with 18 triples. Obviously, he could run. And he was on three pennant winners for the Cubs.

*I*t takes one to know one, so who better to critique 10-time National League All-Star second baseman Ryne Sandberg than four-time National League All-Star second baseman Davey Lopes? Not only were they opponents, contemporaries, and colleagues, they were also teammates briefly with the Cubs.

When Lopes was traded to the Cubs during the 1984 season and joined forces with Sandberg, it was two worlds colliding, the past meeting up with the future.

At the time, Lopes was 39 years old and in the 14th year of a brilliant 16-year major league career in which he would bat .263, steal 557 bases, and have a fielding percentage of .978 in more than 1,400 games at second base. He had already done it all: four All-Star selections, a Gold Glove, a two-time stolen-base champion.

Sandberg was just getting started. He was 24 and in his third season with the Cubs. That season he would win his second of nine consecutive Gold Gloves, make the All-Star team for the first time to start a string of 10 straight years as an All-Star, and be named the National League Most Valuable Player.

"In 1985, I had the best year I ever had stealing bases," said Sandberg. "That was because of Davey's influence. He was such a great base stealer, and he taught me a lot about stealing bases. He was sort of my unofficial base-stealing coach."

Sandberg, who had stolen 37 bases in 1983 and 32 in 1984, jumped to 54 steals, fourth in the league, under Lopes' tutelage. The following season, Sandberg stole 34 bases, but Lopes was traded to Houston in July. With Lopes gone, Sandberg never again stole more than 25 bases.

In 1985, at age 40, Lopes played in 79 games in the outfield for the Cubs, 4 at third base, and only 1 at his normal position, second base, partly out of deference to his age, but largely because Sandberg was solidly entrenched as the Cubs' second baseman.

"Ryno did everything well," Lopes said. "He's one of the best second basemen that ever put on a uniform.

"He was outstanding defensively, but if you mention Ryne Sandberg's name, most people will think offense. He had power; he ran well; he stole bases. He won Gold Gloves, but people will think of Ryno as an offensive-type player, and that's what got him elected to the Hall of Fame.

"When I first saw Sandberg, there wasn't one particular thing that he did that impressed me. I just recognized the fact that he was a good young second baseman at the time. When I got to Chicago, Sandberg was already established. He was an All-Star second baseman for a few years, and he was well on his way to the Hall of Fame. I wouldn't say there was any bond between us because we were both second basemen, but there was the respect factor. You respect what the other guy did in front of you or behind you, whatever the case may be.

"As a teammate, I liked Ryno. He was kind of quiet, but he was a guy who would instigate things and then run away and hide and laugh. He was sneaky. He didn't like practical jokes to be played on him, but he liked playing them on other people. He would start a conversation and instigate something and get a bunch of guys arguing, and all of a sudden you'd look up and Ryno would be over in the corner laughing."

31

Defensively, Herman led the league in putouts by a second baseman seven times, and he led National League second basemen in assists three times and fielding average three times. In six seasons, 1932, 1935, 1938, and 1939 with the Cubs and 1942 and 1943 with Brooklyn, he didn't miss a game. In two other seasons, 1933 and 1936 with the Cubs, he missed only one game. No wonder he's in the Hall of Fame.

My roommate **Glenn Beckert** is one of the funniest guys I ever knew. Great one-liners. One of the best. He'd come up with them out of nowhere, and you'd die laughing. And not all of them were intentional.

Beck was a smoker, but he didn't like to carry cigarettes, and that meant he was constantly bumming smokes. Because I was his roommate, I was an obvious and frequent target. He'd say, "Hey, roomie, you got a cigarette?"

"Why don't you buy your own?" I'd tell him.

And he'd say, "I just don't like to carry them."

Hall of Famer Herman had a lifetime batting average of .304 and was—in the eyes of Leo Durocher, at least—the perfect No. 2 hitter. *Photo courtesy of AP/Wide World Photos.*

Then one day I decided to quit smoking. I wasn't much of a smoker, anyway. I smoked only during the season. A pack of cigarettes would last me a few days, and I was giving most of them to Beck. So I quit smoking, but I told Yosh Kawano, the clubhouse man, "Yosh, put a carton of Winston cigarettes in my roomie's locker, and I'll pay for them."

Yosh put the carton in Beckert's locker, and Beck gave it back to me and said, "I don't want these."

"I quit smoking," I said. "I'm not going to be carrying any more cigarettes."

"You gotta carry them," he said. "You don't have to smoke them, just carry them."

Beck was a guy who got so involved in what was on his mind that he was unaware of things going on around him. Our clubhouse in Wrigley Field was tiny. We had two little sinks for shaving, and you had to walk past two guys shaving to get to the trainer's room. If you weren't careful, you could hit somebody and he could cut himself. It became automatic that any time Beck walked through there, he would run into guys. So if guys were shaving and they'd see Beck coming, they'd immediately put their razors down to avoid getting cut because of him.

One time we went to a black-tie banquet, and sitting at our table was a woman wearing a beautiful white mink. There was a bottle of red wine on the table, and we were sitting at the table when all of a sudden the music started playing. Beck turned to listen to the music, and as he did, he knocked

Beck was one of those guys who was willing to take a hit around second base, this time from Pittsburgh catcher Manny Sanguillen. *Photo courtesy of Time Life Pictures/Getty Images.*

the bottle of red wine all over this woman's beautiful white mink. And Beckert said, "Roomie, did you see that? How about this music?"

On the double play, Beckert wasn't one of those guys who'd get the ball and get out of there. He was tough, and fearless. He'd stand in there and take the hit. People don't realize how good a player Beck was. He was fundamentally sound and a team player. He'd give himself up, move runners along, hit behind the runner—all the things that don't show up in the box score but do help your team win.

He wasn't even aware that he had knocked the wine onto the woman's mink.

As a player, Beckert was greatly underrated, maybe because he was overshadowed by other second basemen at the time, like Bill Mazeroski and Joe Morgan; maybe it was because he never put up big offensive numbers. He was a lifetime .283 hitter, but he never drove in more than 59 runs in a season, and he hit only 22 home runs in 11 years.

But let me tell you, he was a terrific player. He was the ideal two-hole hitter. He could run and hit the ball the other way, and he always made contact. One year, 1968, he struck out only 20 times in 643 at-bats. Five times, he was the toughest batter in the National League to strike out.

Beck came up as a shortstop, then when poor Kenny Hubbs was killed in an airplane crash, they moved Beckert to second base, and he became one of the best in the game. He teamed with Don Kessinger for nine years to form one of the best double-play combinations in the National League.

On the double play, Beckert wasn't one of those guys who'd get the ball and get out of there. He was tough, and fearless. He'd stand in there and take the hit. People don't realize how good a player Beck was. He was fundamentally sound and a team player. He'd give himself up, move runners along, hit behind the runner—all the things that don't show up in the box score but do help your team win.

Johnny Evers was the middleman, and reportedly the brains, of the Cubs' famed double-play combination of Tinker-to-Evers-to-Chance, immortalized in Franklin P. Adams' classic poem, "Baseball's Sad Lexicon" (see the chapter on shortstops).

Shortstop Joe Tinker and first baseman Frank Chance were already in place when Evers, known as "the Crab" for his close-to-the-ground style of fielding ground balls, replaced aging slugger Bobby Lowe at second base in 1903. The trio of Tinker, Evers, and Chance remained a unit for 10 seasons.

Evers was supposedly the brains of the Cubs' legendary double-play combination of the early 1900s, and a star in the team's last World Series win. *Photo courtesy of AP/Wide World Photos.*

Based on their precision and smooth play around second base, one would imagine that Evers and Tinker were the closest of friends, inseparable off the field. In fact, they were hardly that. One day in 1905, the two Cubs got into an argument over cab fare (probably incited by the penurious Tinker). The dispute escalated into a fistfight on the field and several punch-trading incidents in the clubhouse. As a result, the two players did not speak for the remainder of their time together in Chicago.

It took more than three decades for the two to bury the hatchet. Unbeknownst to both, Tinker and Evers were invited to be guest analysts for the radio broadcast of the Cubs' World Series against the Yankees in 1938. When they spotted one another, there was a momentary icy silence. Then they embraced and tears streamed down the cheeks of both men.

Evers was a lifetime .270 batter who hit only 12 home runs in 6,134 at-bats. His best season was 1912 when he batted .341, fourth in the National League behind teammate Heinie Zimmerman. Evers excelled in clutch situations. He batted .350 in both the 1907 and 1908 World Series and knocked in the winning run in the fifth game of the 1908 Series that clinched the Cubs' last world championship. Six years later, playing for Boston, Evers batted .438 in the "Miracle Braves" four-game World Series sweep of the Philadelphia Athletics and drove in the winning run in the 3–1 victory that clinched the championship.

Like his double-play partner Tinker, Evers took his turn as manager of the Cubs, also without much success (Frank Chance also managed the Cubs for eight seasons but with great success). Evers guided the Cubs to a third-place finish in 1913 and a seventh-place finish in 1921. He later managed the White Sox in 1924 and finished eighth.

Evers' reputation as an intelligent, quick-thinking player was based largely on one play, one of the most storied and controversial in baseball history. It came on September 23, 1908, in New York's Polo Grounds with the Cubs, Giants, and Pirates engaged in one of the tightest pennant races ever.

The Giants and Cubs went to the bottom of the ninth tied, 1–1, when with two outs and runners on first and third, Al Bridwell singled home Mike McCormick from third to give the Giants an apparent 2–1 victory. Giants rookie Fred Merkle, the runner on first, failed to touch second base. When the ball dropped safely, and once McCormick had scored, Merkle simply stopped running and headed for the clubhouse, which was the accepted, if illegal, practice of the day.

Ever alert, Evers called for the ball and stepped on second base to record the third out. Umpire Hank O'Day ruled Merkle out, nullifying the winning run. The game was declared a tie. When the Cubs and Giants finished deadlocked for the pennant, it necessitated a replay of the tie game to determine the National League pennant winner. The Cubs won the playoff and the pennant and went on to beat Detroit in the World Series.

Because of "Merkle's boner," and Evers' quick thinking, the Giants were denied a pennant and the Cubs won the World Series. They haven't won one since.

I had the pleasure of meeting the great **Rogers Hornsby**, who baseball historians say was the greatest right-handed hitter in the history of the game. I mean the man once batted .424 for an entire season. Are you kidding me? His lifetime batting average was .358. And he hit home runs. He hit 301 homers for his career and led the league with 42 in 1922 when the second man hit 26. You looked at this man, not a very big man, about 5'11", 175 or 180 pounds, and you said to yourself, "How could he have been that good?"

The reason I don't put him higher on my list of Cubs second basemen is that he played only four seasons for them.

Hornsby played most of his career—the first 13 years—with the St. Louis Cardinals and managed them in 1925 and 1926, when he won the World Series with many of the players who formed the famed Gashouse Gang of the thirties. The following year, he was traded to the Giants, where he stayed only one year and was traded to the Braves. After one year in Boston, the Cubs got him for $200,000—a king's ransom in those days—and five players.

In 1929, his first year with the Cubs, Hornsby batted .380, hit 39 home runs, drove in 149 runs, won his second Most Valuable Player award, and

37

The great Hornsby played only four seasons for the Cubs, but his MVP season of 1929 (.380 average, 39 home runs, 149 RBIs) rates as one of the best in club history. *Photo courtesy of AP/Wide World Photos.*

helped the Cubs win their first pennant in 11 years. He missed most of the 1930 season with a broken leg but came back as player/manager when Joe McCarthy was fired. He led the Cubs to a second-place finish in 1930 and third in 1931. Midway through the 1932 season, with the team in second place, Hornsby was fired by the Cubs and replaced by my old friend, Charlie Grimm.

Hornsby finished out his 23-year career in St. Louis, with the Cardinals and Browns.

The reason Hornsby moved around so much is that he was a cantankerous sort—insubordinate, contentious, outspoken, and disagreeable. But I can honestly say I never saw any of that from him when I met him. I had just signed with the Cubs and was invited to a three-week camp for Cubs prospects in Arizona in February of 1959. Rogers was the Cubs' minor league hitting instructor, and he ran that camp.

I used to bat with my front foot even with the front part of the plate. Hornsby watched me hit for a couple of days, and he had only one suggestion. "Ron," he said, "I wouldn't change a thing. You're going to be a big leaguer, no doubt about it, but I would move back to the back line because that will help you pick up the breaking ball better. And that's all I recommend."

I was only 19 years old at the time, so you can imagine how I felt being a right-handed hitter and those words coming from Rogers Hornsby, the greatest right-handed hitter who ever lived.

At the end of the three-week camp, we were all sitting on a picnic bench. There were two lines—about 10, 11 pitchers, and the rest were all prospects. And here came Hornsby. He went down the line and had a comment for each prospect. He came to the first line and said to one guy, "You might as well go home now because you won't get past A ball."

He went down the whole first line, and with each guy he came to he had nothing good to say. Billy Williams and I were sitting in the second line, and I was listening to him criticize everybody, and I was thinking, "Is he going to say that to us?" Even though he had told both Billy and me that he thought we would be big leaguers, you never know. He had demolished that entire first row.

Hornsby came to our row, and there was one guy ahead of Billy and me. Hornsby looked him in the eye and said, "You *may* get to Double A."

Now he came to Billy. "You," Hornsby said, "can play in the big leagues right now."

I was next, and my heart was pounding, and I was thinking, "Please, please, don't tell me to go home."

And he said, "You are going to play in the big leagues."

There must have been 30 prospects in that camp, and Billy and I were the only ones Hornsby predicted would play in the big leagues . . . and we were the only 2 of the 30 who did.

I had heard there was another side to him, but we never saw it. He was great with us. In fact, when Billy and I went to the big leagues, we were struggling a little bit and the Cubs' general manager called Hornsby to take a look at us. Naturally there was no videotape in those days. All we had was 16-millimeter film, and Hornsby took it and studied it and right away he picked up a flaw. He was a guy who didn't make things complicated. All he told me was, "For some reason you're dropping your back shoulder a little bit. Hitting is all even. The shoulders should be even."

I don't know anything about the problems he had when he was a player, but my impression of Hornsby is that he loved the game of baseball, and he was very helpful to me when I was a young ballplayer. I have always believed that you have to judge a person by the way he treats you, and Rogers Hornsby was very good to me at a time when I needed encouragement and support, so I have nothing but good things to say about him.

Statistical Summaries

All statistics are for player's Cubs career only.

HITTING

G = Games

H = Hits

HR = Home runs

RBI = Runs batted in

SB = Stolen bases

BA = Batting average

Second Baseman	Years	G	H	HR	RBI	SB	BA
Ryne Sandberg *Had hits in eight consecutive at-bats in 1992*	1982–94 1996–97	2,151	2,385	282	1,061	344	.285
Billy Herman *Holds record for most putouts by a second baseman in a season (466 in 1933)*	1931–41	1,344	1,710	37	577	53	.309

continued	Years	G	H	HR	RBI	SB	BA
Glenn Beckert *Had a 27-game hitting streak in 1968*	1965–73	1,247	1,423	22	353	49	.283
Johnny Evers *Stole home 21 times during his career*	1902–13	1,409	1,340	9	448	291	.276
Rogers Hornsby *Had career-high 156 runs scored in 1929*	1929–32	317	392	58	264	3	.350

FIELDING

PO = Putouts

A = Assists

E = Errors

DP = Double plays

TC/G = Total chances divided by games played

FA = Fielding average

Second Baseman	PO	A	E	DP	TC/G	FA
Ryne Sandberg	3,806	6,361	109	1,157	5.2	.989
Billy Herman	3,658	4,453	285	918	6.3	.966
Glenn Beckert	2,640	3,632	169	742	5.3	.974
Johnny Evers	3,072	4,130	369	525	5.5	.951
Rogers Hornsby	437	828	50	146	5.3	.962

FOUR

Shortstop

I HAVE ALREADY DEALT WITH **Ernie Banks**, "Mr. Cub," in the chapter on first basemen and told you how great he was as a hitter and how much admiration and affection I have for him as a man. Now I'll deal with him as a shortstop and why I believe he deserves to be rated the No. 1 Cub at two positions.

Younger fans that remember him as a first baseman might find it hard to believe Ernie played almost as many games at shortstop (1,125) as he did at first base (1,259). He made the All-Star team seven times as a shortstop and won his back-to-back MVPs, in 1958 and 1959, as a shortstop.

By the time I came to the Cubs in 1960, Ernie was in his eighth season as their shortstop. I got to play alongside

1. ERNIE BANKS

2. BILLY JURGES

3. DON KESSINGER

4. JOE TINKER

5. SHAWON DUNSTON

him for my first two seasons before he moved to first base. Before I got there, they tell me he was erratic. In 1958, he led the league in errors with 32, but typical of Ernie, he worked hard to improve and the next year he set a record for shortstops by making only 12 errors all season. He led National League shortstops in fielding in 1960 and 1961 and won a Gold Glove in 1960.

Typical of Ernie, after leading NL shortstops with 32 errors in 1958 (he was still voted MVP), he worked hard and came back the next year with a record-few 12 errors (and another MVP award). *Photo courtesy of AP/Wide World Photos.*

44

By the time I got to see him, injuries to his legs had cut down on his range, but anything hit to him he would pick up with those soft hands that made him so good at digging balls out of the dirt at first base. Eventually, his leg injuries were the reason he was moved to first base, which probably added years to his career.

Ernie actually hit more home runs as a shortstop—a National League record 277—than he did as a first baseman (235), and the 47 homers he hit in 1958 is still the National League record for home runs by a shortstop, which makes his choice as the No. 1 shortstop in Cubs history a no-brainer.

*T*o look at Len Merullo playing shortstop for the Cubs in the forties was to see a mirror image of Billy Jurges: same size (Jurges 5'11", 175 pounds; Merullo 5'11½", 166 pounds), same way of running on the tiptoes, same spread-out, open batting stance. It was no accident and no coincidence.

"He was my idol," said Merullo. "If ever a guy was a boy's hero, it was Jurgy. He was my hero. I copied him to a T—the way he moved around, the way he batted. I wore my uniform the way he did. I rolled my pants up just the way he rolled his. I even copied his habit of taking the gum out of his mouth when he went up to bat and putting it on the knob of his cap."

Born in Boston, Merullo became a Cubs fan at a young age.

"There was a man named Ralph Wheeler, who was Mr. Baseball in our area," he remembered. "He covered high school sports for the *Boston Herald*, and he was a Cubs fan. He had a relationship with the Cubs, and he would bring ballplayers to Braves Field when the Cubs played there, and they would work out with the team. You'd get into one of those old, baggy uniforms, and you'd go out and the coaches would give you a workout."

It was at one of those workouts that Merullo first spotted the man who became his idol and who was nine years older than Merullo, almost to the day (Jurges born May 9, 1908; Merullo May 5, 1917). By the time Merullo reached Chicago in 1941, Jurges had been traded to the Giants, but he returned to the Cubs in 1946 for the final two years of his career, and Merullo got to be teammates with his idol.

"I used to blame him for the problems I had as a hitter," said Merullo. "I copied everything about him, but the one thing I wish I didn't copy was the way he hit [Jurges was a lifetime .258 hitter with 43 homers and 656 RBIs for 1,816 games; Merullo batted .240 with 6 homers and 152 RBIs in 639 games].

"Jurgy wasn't much of a hitter, but he was a hell of a fielder with speed and a great arm. He played shortstop the way it should be played, and he and Billy Herman at second base were as good a double-play combination as there was in baseball at the time."

Merullo became the Cubs' regular shortstop in 1942, and he was the shortstop for the last Cubs team to play in the World Series, in 1945. Admittedly

45

a weak hitter, Merullo was a slick fielder except for one memorable day. On the day his son, Len Jr., was born, Merullo committed four errors. To prove he had a sense of humor, Merullo nicknamed the boy "Boots."

When his playing career was over, Merullo remained with the Cubs as a scout, a position he held for 25 years until he joined Major League Baseball's central scouting bureau. In 2002, at the age of 85, Len Merullo retired to his home in Reading, Massachusetts, having spent 63 consecutive years in baseball.

If you saw the movie *The Natural*, with Robert Redford as the slugger Roy Hobbs, you no doubt remember the scene where a crazed woman goes to Hobbs' hotel room and shoots him, almost ending his career. This actually happened to not one, but two Cubs players (wouldn't you know such a thing would happen to the Cubs?). Eddie Waitkus, a Cubs first baseman in the forties, and **Billy Jurges**, No. 2 on my all-time list of Cubs shortstops, were the unfortunate shooting victims.

In Jurges' case, it happened in July of 1932, soon after he had taken over from Woody English as the Cubs shortstop. The story goes that a woman called Jurges in his hotel room and then entered the room with a gun and threatened to commit suicide. In an attempt to stop her, the gun went off, and Jurges took one bullet in his hand and another through his ribs.

Fortunately, the wounds were just superficial and Jurges would miss only three weeks. However, the shooting set off a chain reaction that would lead to one of the most famous moments in baseball history.

With the Cubs battling for the pennant and the uncertainty of Jurges' status, veteran former Yankees shortstop Mark Koenig was brought to Chicago to fill in for Jurges. Koenig performed admirably, batting .353 in 33 games and helping the Cubs win the pennant. Despite his important contribution, Koenig's teammates voted him only a one-half World Series share. The Cubs' shabby treatment of Koenig drew the wrath of his former Yankees teammates, notably Babe Ruth, who let them know of his feelings. Throughout the 1932 World Series, Ruth continually carped at the Cubs, calling them cheapskates and ingrates. And the Cubs fired right back at the mighty Babe.

This back-and-forth jockeying came to a head in the fifth inning of Game 3 in Chicago. With Charlie Root on the mound for the Cubs, and the Chicago bench giving the Babe a thorough going-over, Ruth came to bat with the score tied, 4–4. What is fact is that Ruth pointed at the center-field fence, took a strike, pointed again, and then hit the next pitch right where he had pointed for his second home run of the game.

Did Ruth actually call his home run? It depends on whose story you believe. Ruth, himself, kept the controversy going and never really said for sure one way or the other. At times he hinted that he did point. Other times he denied that he pointed.

According to Charlie Grimm, the Cubs' manager at the time, Ruth was being needled from the bench by Cubs pitcher Guy Bush, and Babe was reacting to the bench-jockeying of Bush, pointing to the pitcher's mound and saying, "You'll be out there tomorrow."

Jurges is probably better known for his unfortunate role in one of the strangest baseball stories of all time than for his considerable talents as a shortstop. *Photo courtesy of AP/Wide World Photos.*

Bush did start for the Cubs the next day and lasted just one-third of an inning. When he faced Ruth, he hit him with a pitch. The Yankees scored four in the first and rolled to a 13–6 victory to complete a four-game sweep of the Cubs.

Jurges, the innocent bystander to all these memorable events, had reclaimed his shortstop job from Koenig and batted .364 in the World Series. He then went on to have six productive years for the Cubs before being traded to the New York Giants.

In Chicago, Jurges teamed with second baseman Billy Herman to give the Cubs the National League's top double-play combination and helped guide the Cubs to three pennants. Jurges, a New York native who attended the same high school as Hall of Famer Phil Rizzuto, led National League short-stops in fielding percentage four times and once collected nine consecutive hits, one short of the National League record.

Jurges returned to the Cubs to finish out the last two years of his playing career, and then he became a Cubs coach. He later managed the Red Sox for parts of two seasons. His record as a manager was undistinguished, except for one fact. With Jurges as manager in 1959, 12 years after Jackie Robinson broke the major leagues' color barrier, Pumpsie Green joined the Red Sox, ending their dubious distinction as the last team in the major leagues without a black player.

Whatever success I may have had as a third baseman in the major leagues, I owe a lot of it to **Don Kessinger**. He was my security blanket. By that I mean as a third baseman, feeling secure at your position has a lot to do with your success. If you know your shortstop can go into the hole and come up with the ball and throw out a fast runner, that gives you security. And that's what I had with Kesh.

I'll give you an example. Curt Flood of the Cardinals was a great ballplayer and a very fast runner who got out of the box quickly. I've seen Kessinger go in the hole, make a backhanded pickup, and then come up in the air and throw Flood out. That's hard to do, but Kessinger did it a lot. My point is Kesh had great range. He could turn the double play. And he made my job easier.

As a third baseman, I always felt that the majority of the hits are in the hole between short and third, but with Kesh, if he moved to his left for a left-handed hitter, I would move a step or two toward the hole. But with a right-handed hitter up, I could favor the line and I could still get to a lot of balls going to my left. And what I couldn't get, I knew he could. We cut off a lot of hits playing that way.

Kessinger was the best I ever played with. When he took over at shortstop, I had been with the Cubs five years and Kesh solidified our infield. He wasn't flashy, but he was steady. He made the plays a shortstop has to make.

In his first season with the Cubs, Kessinger led National League shortstops in errors. But he worked hard to improve and soon became one of the best defensive shortstops in the league. He was the National League's starting shortstop in the All-Star Game five times. He led the league in putouts for a shortstop three times, in assists and double plays four times, and in fielding percentage once. And, in 1969, he set a then–major league record for short-stops with 54 straight errorless games.

Another of my old teammates, Kesh had great range at shortstop, which took a lot of pressure off me on those ground balls into the hole. *Photo courtesy of Bettmann/ CORBIS.*

Tinker was not exactly a fearsome figure at the plate, but he was the centerpiece for one of the most storied infields in baseball history. *Photo courtesy of AP/Wide World Photos.*

Donnie also made himself into a good offensive player. He had been strictly a right-handed hitter in the minor leagues, but he taught himself to be a switch-hitter once he got to the big leagues, and he became our leadoff hitter, and a good one.

Kessinger was tall and thin, 6'1" and 170 pounds. I remember when he first came up, Leo Durocher said, "You're going to have to plug the drains in the shower so he doesn't slip through." He looked fragile, but he wasn't. He played 16 seasons in the big leagues and had 1,931 hits. In one game, he was six for six.

On the surface, his career record—a .263 batting average, 31 home runs, 782 RBIs in 15 seasons—would not seem to merit **Joe Tinker**'s inclusion in the Hall of Fame. However, there are other factors to consider.

In 11 seasons as the Cubs' shortstop, Tinker led the league in fielding percentage four times, in chances accepted three times, and in putouts and assists twice each.

Tinker was the centerpiece of an infield, including Harry Steinfeldt at third, Johnny Evers at second, and Frank Chance at first, that brought new focus to inner defense in baseball and devised strategies designed to defeat the stolen base, the hit-and-run, and the bunt, including the rotation play still in use today.

With Tinker as their shortstop, the Cubs attained the greatest success in their history, winning three consecutive National League pennants (1906–08), four in five years (1910), and their last two World Series (1907 and 1908).

And there's the poem:

> *These are the saddest of possible words,*
> *"Tinker to Evers to Chance."*
> *Trio of bear cubs and fleeter than birds,*
> *"Tinker to Evers to Chance."*
> *Ruthlessly pricking our gonfalon bubble,*
> *Making a Giant hit into a double,*
> *Words that are weighty with nothing but trouble.*
> *"Tinker to Evers to Chance."*

There are conflicting stories about the time and place of origin of the poem, first titled "That Double Play Again?" later changed to "Baseball's Sad Lexicon," and popularly known as "Tinker to Evers to Chance."

51

It first appeared in either the *New York Globe* on July 10, 1908, or the *New York Evening Mail* on July 10, 1910. What seems to be fact is that the poet, Franklin P. Adams, was informed by his editor that his newspaper column was eight lines short. On his way to cover a game between the New York Giants and Chicago Cubs at the Polo Grounds, Adams penned the eight lines that became, next to "Casey at the Bat," the most famous of all baseball poems.

When Shawon Dunston went across the white lines, nobody was his friend. He played the game the way it should be played. I liked that about him. He was a funny man, a good guy to be around. He enjoyed baseball, and he loved people.

There is no doubt that the popularity of the poem, and the attention it brought to the Cubs' double-play combination, led to their induction in baseball's Hall of Fame, particularly in the case of Tinker and Evers. That theory is supported by the fact that Tinker, Evers, and Chance were elected in the same year, 1946.

Ironically, in the 10 years they were together, the Cubs never led the National League in double plays.

Offensively, Tinker was not a feared batsman, although throughout his career he maintained a mystical ability to hit the great Christy Mathewson. Against the legendary New York Giants pitcher, "Big Six," Tinker batted almost 100 points higher than his career average. Tinker's greatest asset on offense was his speed and ability to steal bases. He averaged 28 stolen bases a season for the Cubs, and on July 28, 1910, he tied a major league record by stealing home twice in one game.

Had he come along several decades later, Tinker might have attained fame for another reason. He might have been the Curt Flood of his day.

Far ahead of his time, Tinker was a staunch advocate for players' rights and railed against team owners' penny-pinching of players, primarily himself. In 1909, he demanded a $1,000 raise from his salary of $1,500 and sat out part of the season before settling for an increase of $200.

After the 1912 season, Tinker was traded by the Cubs to Cincinnati, where his battle with ownership and his demand for more money continued, prompting the Reds to sell him to Brooklyn. Tinker refused to play for either team unless he received $10,000 of the $25,000 sale price. Here's a player Marvin Miller would have loved.

When the Reds failed to meet his demand, Tinker jumped to the outlaw Federal League as player/manager of the Chicago Whales.

Dunston, the hugely hyped first pick in the 1982 draft, could do things at shortstop that Cubs fans had never seen before. *Photo courtesy of AP/Wide World Photos.*

Tinker returned to the Cubs as manager in 1916, finished a disappointing fifth, and was dismissed, but he continued to be involved in baseball in a variety of roles: minor league manager, minor league team owner, and scout. Tinker Field in Orlando, the longtime spring training home of the Minnesota Twins, was named for the Cubs shortstop who was immortalized in poem.

Shawon Dunston was the complete opposite of Don Kessinger. Shawon made the difficult plays—some of the most fantastic plays you'll ever see. For some reason, I don't know why, he had problems with routine plays.

Dunston had one of the best—if not the best—arms I've ever seen for a shortstop.

When Shawon went across the white lines, nobody was his friend. He played the game the way it should be played. I liked that about him. He was a funny man, a good guy to be around. He enjoyed baseball, and he loved people.

People always said he could have been better, and maybe he could have. But he had a long career—18 years, the first 11 with the Cubs. And he finished with a lifetime batting average of .269, 150 home runs, 668 RBIs, and 212 stolen bases.

That's good enough to make my top five, but because he was the No. 1 draft pick in the country in 1982, people expected a lot more from him.

Statistical Summaries

All statistics are for player's Cubs career only.

HITTING

G = Games

H = Hits

HR = Home runs

RBI = Runs batted in

SB = Stolen bases

BA = Batting average

Shortstop	Years	G	H	HR	RBI	SB	BA
Ernie Banks *Led NL in extra-base hits four times (1955, 1957, 1958, 1960)*	1953–71	2,528	2,583	512	1,636	50	.274
Billy Jurges *Led NL shortstops in putouts, assists, double plays, and fielding percentage in 1935*	1931–38 1946–47	1,072	928	20	390	22	.254

continued	Years	G	H	HR	RBI	SB	BA
Don Kessinger *Went 6-for-6 on June 17, 1971*	1964–75	1,648	1,619	11	431	92	.255
Joe Tinker *Hit Cubs' first-ever World Series home run in 1908 (Game 2)*	1902–13 1916	1,537	1,436	28	670	304	.259
Shawon Dunston *Hit three triples on July 28, 1990*	1985–95 1997	1,254	1,219	107	489	175	.267

FIELDING

PO = Putouts

A = Assists

E = Errors

DP = Double plays

TC/G = Total chances divided by games played

FA = Fielding average

Shortstop	PO	A	E	DP	TC/G	FA
Ernie Banks	2,087	3,441	174	724	5.1	.969
Billy Jurges	1,995	3,098	195	598	5.5	.963
Don Kessinger	2,642	5,346	296	982	5.1	.964
Joe Tinker	3,248	5,083	574	584	5.9	.936
Shawon Dunston	2,114	3,416	183	641	5.1	.968

FIVE

Third Baseman

WHO COULD BLAME CUBS FANS for being confused when the 1932 season began? One Hack was gone, and another Hack was beginning a distinguished career with the Cubs that lasted 16 years, which, at the time, tied a National League record for most years as a third baseman.

In December of 1931, slugger Hack Wilson, who had blasted 190 home runs in six seasons on Chicago's North Side, including a then–National League record 56 in 1930 to go along with his still major league record 191 RBIs, had been traded to the Cardinals for the old spitballer Burleigh Grimes. And **Stan Hack** arrived as the heir apparent to Woody English as the Cubs' third baseman.

Known as "Smiling Stan" for his cheery disposition and perpetual smile, Hack would play his entire career with the Cubs and emerge as one of their most popular players.

1. STAN HACK

2. BILL MADLOCK

3. ARAMIS RAMIREZ

4. NED WILLIAMSON

5. WOODY ENGLISH

An opposing player once said that Hack "has more friends than Leo Durocher has enemies," and Bill Veeck once used Hack's smile as a promotion. Veeck roamed the Wrigley Field bleachers selling a picture of a smiling Hack on the back of a mirror that had the slogan, "Smile with Stan Hack."

Hack (on the far right, smiling) was not the prototypical third baseman of his day, but he was a five-time All-Star who finished with a .301 career batting average. *Photo courtesy of AP/Wide World Photos.*

I met Stan Hack, and I was surprised when I saw him. I had heard a lot about him, and before I met him, I visualized him differently. He wasn't a big man—about 6', 170 pounds—and he didn't hit home runs. He wasn't the prototypical third baseman of his day, but he could pick it at third base and hit for average. A heckuva ballplayer. He was a left-handed hitter who batted leadoff. He was a line-drive hitter, and a good one. He had a lifetime average of .301 and 2,193 hits. He hit .300 six times, made the All-Star team five times, scored 100 runs or more seven times, led the league in stolen bases twice and in hits twice, and played on four pennant winners with the Cubs.

In the field, he twice led the league in fielding and assists, and five times in putouts.

Hack retired after the 1943 season, but when his favorite manager, Charlie Grimm, was brought back to manage the Cubs 11 games into the 1944 season, Hack was coaxed out of retirement. He batted .282 in 98 games for the Cubs in 1944, and the following season batted .323 and helped the Cubs win their last pennant.

Later, Hack managed the Cubs, but without success. In his three seasons as manager, the Cubs never finished higher than sixth.

Bill Madlock, "Mad Dog," was a Cub only three years, so he might not deserve to be rated as high as No. 2 among Cubs' third basemen. But look at what he did in those three years.

The Cubs got him from Texas in a trade for Fergie Jenkins, and Mad Dog replaced me at third base. In his first year as a Cub, Madlock batted .313. Then he won back-to-back batting championships with a .354 average in 1975 and .339 in 1976. He later won two more batting titles with the Pirates, the only player in baseball history to win more than one batting championship with two different teams.

He didn't hit for a lot of power, and I didn't see enough of him to judge his defense. But what a hitter! He had a beautiful swing, and he was another guy who when he went across the white lines was all baseball.

59

Two of the best hitters—and hard-nosed ballplayers—of my era (and quite a bit later): Madlock (left) and Pete Rose. *Photo courtesy of Bettmann/CORBIS.*

At his young age, and based on what he's accomplished so far, it's my prediction that Ramirez will wind up at the top of the list of all-time Cubs third basemen. *Photo courtesy of AP/Wide World Photos.*

Aramis Ramirez is another guy, like Bill Madlock, who came in a trade and who has been with the Cubs only a short time, but at his age (he turned 26 on June 25, 2004) and with what he has accomplished already, I predict that before he's through, if he stays healthy, he will become one of the best third basemen in the game and will go to the top of the list of Cubs third basemen.

What a steal it was for the Cubs when they got Ramirez from the Pirates in a five-player trade midway through the 2003 season. At the time of the trade, the Cubs were in third place, four and a half games behind the Astros in the National League Central. After the trade, they won 38 of their last 63 games and finished one game ahead of Houston.

The Cubs were looking for a leadoff hitter, and the key player for them in the trade was Kenny Lofton, who filled that role and turned the Cubs' season around by batting .327, stealing 12 bases, and scoring 39 runs in 56 games.

A third baseman has to stay alert and keep his head in the game. He can't relax because he never knows when a ball will be hit his way. And Aramis Ramirez is a guy who's always in the game. He has the perfect mentality and demeanor to play the position, and he has the talent to be a franchise player.

The Cubs would not have won the division without Lofton, and they might not have won it without Aramis Ramirez. He had had a big year for the Pirates in 2001 when he batted .300, hit 34 home runs, and drove in 112 at the age of 23, and the only reason he was included in the deal was that the Pirates felt they could not afford him.

At first, Ramirez struggled a little when he got to Chicago (that often happens to a young player when he gets traded), but he wound up hitting 15 homers and driving in 39 runs in 63 games, and then he hit three homers and drove in seven runs in the League Championship Series against Florida.

In 2004, Ramirez had a breakout season with the Cubs. He batted .318 with 36 homers and 103 RBIs, and I truly believe he was their MVP. He's what you call a four-tool player. He can hit, hit for power, field, and throw. The one thing he doesn't do well is run. I don't mean he's a slow runner, but he's not a guy who's going to steal a lot of bases. He's someone who hits for power and average, and he doesn't strike out much (only 62 times in 547 at-bats in 2004). He's a good contact hitter who goes to the plate knowing he has the pitcher in trouble. That's what good hitters do.

A lot of hitters get uptight at the plate, but not Ramirez. He's one of the few hitters you see these days who goes up there with an idea.

Defensively, he's outstanding, and he's getting better. I didn't get to see a lot of him when he was in Pittsburgh, but the knock on him was that he made a lot of errors. To me, it isn't how many errors you make; it's how many assists you get. In 2003 Ramirez had 33 errors, but he also had 336 assists. In 2004 he had only 10 errors, so you could say he improved his defense. But he had only 221 assists, 115 less than the previous year. So I ask you, was he a better third baseman in 2004, when he had only 10 errors, or in 2003, when he got to more balls? I'll take the latter. From 1964 to 1968, I won five consecutive Gold Gloves even though I averaged more than 20 errors a year—but I also averaged 380 assists a year. That means you're getting to balls that maybe other third basemen don't get to.

The thing about being a good third baseman is you have to always be in the game. Playing third base can be boring at times because you may not get a lot of balls hit your way. In my day, there were more hard throwers. Today, there are more finesse pitchers, so a third baseman has to stay alert and keep his head in the game. He can't relax because he never knows when a ball will be hit his way. And Aramis is a guy who's always in the game. He has the perfect mentality and demeanor to play the position, and he has the talent to be a franchise player.

Here's a name that even old timers I've talked to know very little about: **Ned Williamson**. But if you look in the record books, you'll see that the most home runs hit in a season before Babe Ruth came along were by Williamson for the Cubs.

Williamson hit 27 homers in 1884, when home runs were as rare as complete games for pitchers are today. There was a reason for this explosion, but I'll get to that later. Suffice it to say that when Ruth hit 29 home runs for Boston in 1919, Williamson had held the record for 35 years, one year longer than the Babe's record of 60 home runs had lasted until Roger Maris hit 61 in 1961.

The reason for the skepticism regarding Williamson's record is that he did it in Lake Front Park, the bandbox home of the Cubs (White Stockings) from 1878 to 1884 with its short left-field (196 feet) and right-field (180 feet) fences.

The fences were so short the National League established a ground rule that any player hitting a ball over either the left-field or right-field fence would be awarded a two-base hit. That enabled Williamson to set a then–major league record for doubles with 49 in 1883.

here are nine major league third basemen currently enshrined in the Baseball Hall of Fame at Cooperstown, the fewest number of any position, and not one of them is named Ron Santo, which raises one question: why not?

"Oh, yeah, he's a Hall of Famer," said Randy Hundley, a Cubs teammate of Santo's for eight seasons, 1966–73. "Maybe he was overlooked because we had three players on that team go into the Hall of Fame [Ernie Banks, Billy Williams, and Ferguson Jenkins], but that's not fair to Ronnie. When you look at the numbers, they show he belongs. People just have to look at the bloomin' numbers."

Here are the "bloomin' numbers." Santo hit more home runs than seven of the nine third basemen in the Hall of Fame (Frank "Home Run" Baker, George Brett, Jimmy Collins, George Kell, Fred Lindstrom, Brooks Robinson, and Pie Traynor), had more hits than four of the nine (Baker, Collins, Kell, and Lindstrom), had more RBIs than five of the nine (Baker, Collins, Kell, Lindstrom, and Traynor), and had a higher lifetime batting average than three of the nine (Eddie Mathews, Robinson, and Mike Schmidt). Santo is widely regarded as one of the greatest Cub third basemen of all time (although he was too modest to include himself in this book's top-five list).

"There were two third basemen in the National League in my time who should be in the Hall of Fame and aren't," said pitcher Tommy John. "Ken Boyer and Ron Santo. If you look at the numbers, theirs are better than Tony Perez'. Santo was hard to pitch to because he could hit the ball hard to right center. You just had to make sure he didn't start leaning out over the plate, but to pitch inside in Wrigley was hard."

"Santo was an outstanding player," said Hundley. "He was an excellent defensive third baseman and a great hitter. I came up through the Giants' organization, so I never really got to see much of him, except in spring training, until I went to Chicago. I can remember when I joined the Cubs, catching batting practice in spring training when Ronnie was hitting. I had never seen anyone get the bat through the hitting area as quickly as Ronnie. The ball would be past him and all of a sudden, here comes the bat. It was unbelievable to me.

"Ronnie was an excellent teammate, a competitor, and a leader. Leo [Durocher] thought enough of him to make him our captain.

63

If there was one thing about Ronnie it was that he wore his emotions on his sleeve. You always knew what he was thinking. It was right out there. Many times I'd have to duck when he struck out from the helmets being thrown.

"We always used to rag on him when we were playing. There was a lot of banter back and forth on that team, but it was good-natured. I guess I was an instigator because guys would come to me and give me lines to use on Ronnie, like calling him a hypochondriac. I lockered next to him on the road—when we went to visiting ballparks, they would assign us lockers according to our uniform numbers and I was No. 9 and Santo was No. 10—and I never knew he was a diabetic. I played with the guy for six years before I found out. I was ignorant of the disease.

"The first indication I had was one night a ball was hit to him and he bobbled it and threw to first and the umpire called the runner safe on a close play. Ronnie is hollering and screaming and then all of a sudden he goes down on one knee, gets up, and runs into the dugout and gets a Hershey's bar, and I'm thinking, 'What's that all about?'

"I was his teammate and I didn't appreciate what he was going through, and now that I'm aware of what he went through, I realize he accomplished an awful lot.

"There were times he would have blackouts because his sugar would fluctuate so quickly. Once he hit a grand slam and later he said he did it while he was suffering from double vision. When we talked about it, he said hitting the ball wasn't as tough as running around the bases. It was incredible.

"Today, we're still close, and I still rag on him. I always will. I'm grateful for that relationship. I love the guy to death, and I admire him so much.

"Ron is so beloved in Chicago. People care about him. I can't go anywhere without people asking, 'How's Ron doing?' And I'm happy to say he's doing fine. He was beloved as a player and he's beloved today as an announcer. He has motivated a lot of other people because he has such a passion for the Cubs.

"I always tell people you have not played in the big leagues until you've played for the Chicago Cubs, and that's because of the great Cubs fans."

Editor's Note: As this book went to press, members of the Veterans Committee were deliberating Ron Santo's credentials for induction into the Baseball Hall of Fame. But 30 years after he played his last major league game, 15 years after he failed to gain the necessary votes for election from the Baseball Writers Association of America, many of his contemporaries wonder why Santo has so far been denied an honor he richly deserves.

Williamson, (front row, second from left) shown with his teammates in 1885—one year after he hit 27 home runs in the very friendly confines of Lake Front Park. *Photo courtesy of the Rucker Archive.*

The rule was changed in 1884, the White Stockings' last in Lake Front, so that balls hit over any fence would be ruled home runs. The entire Chicago team took great advantage of the change, especially Williamson, who belted his record 27 homers, almost double the existing major league record of 14 hit the previous season by Harry Stovey of Philadelphia in the American Association. Williamson also was the first player ever to hit three home runs in one game.

As a team, the White Stockings blasted 142 home runs, a record that stood until the Murderers' Row Yankees of 1927 hit 158. All but 10 of Chicago's 142 home runs in 1884 were hit at home.

His manager, Cap Anson, called Williamson "the greatest all-around ballplayer the country ever saw." Williamson led the National League in assists seven times, double plays six times, fielding average four times, and putouts twice. And this, remember, was in the days when fielders did not use gloves.

English actually played about twice as many games at shortstop as he did at third base during his Cubs career, but his slick fielding and steady bat helped the Cubs bring home the pennant in 1932. *Photo courtesy of AP/Wide World Photos.*

Woody English played more games at shortstop (826) than he did at third base (400), and he was an outstanding shortstop, good enough to help the Cubs win a pennant in 1929 and lead the National League in putouts two years later. But I'm exercising my prerogative and placing him fourth on my all-time list of Cubs third basemen, where he also excelled.

English's best year at bat came in 1930 when he played more games at third than short. He batted .335, had career highs in home runs with 14 and in RBIs with 59, and was among the league leaders in runs scored, triples, and walks.

English was the Cubs' regular shortstop in 1931, but the following year he again moved to third to make room for Billy Jurges, who was considered the better fielding shortstop. You might say English was the Alex Rodriguez of his day. The move proved to be a great one for the Cubs all around. Jurges led all National League shortstops in fielding percentage; English, who had played the position before, was a solid third baseman; and the Cubs won the pennant.

By 1934, English's days as a Cubs third baseman were numbered. Stan Hack had arrived, and he would win the job and hold it for 16 years.

Statistical Summaries

All statistics are for player's Cubs career only.

HITTING

G = Games

H = Hits

HR = Home runs

RBI = Runs batted in

SB = Stolen bases

BA = Batting average

Third Baseman	Years	G	H	HR	RBI	SB	BA
Stan Hack *Had .348 career World Series average with 24 hits*	1932–47	1,938	2,193	57	642	165	.301
Bill Madlock *Was co-MVP of 1975 All-Star Game*	1974–76	400	498	31	202	35	.336
Aramis Ramirez *Had a pair of three-homer games in 2004 (July 30 and September 16)*	2003–04	208	234	51	152	1	.300

continued	Years	G	H	HR	RBI	SB	BA
Ned Williamson *First player to hit three homers in a game (May 30, 1884)*	1879–89	1,065	1,050	61	622	85	.260
Woody English *Had 314 combined hits and walks in 1930 (214 hits and 100 walks)*	1927–36	1,098	1,248	31	373	51	.291

FIELDING

PO = Putouts

A = Assists

E = Errors

DP = Double plays

TC/G = Total chances divided by games played

FA = Fielding average

Third Baseman	PO	A	E	DP	TC/G	FA
Stan Hack	1,944	3,494	246	255	3.1	.957
Bill Madlock	270	713	52	49	2.7	.950
Aramis Ramirez	127	341	20	29	2.4	.959
Ned Williamson	737	1,500	334	107	4.3	.870
Woody English	375	704	36	54	2.9	.968

SIX

Left Fielder

I HAVE KNOWN **Billy Williams** longer than I've known anybody else in baseball, almost 50 years. I first met him when we were both kids. I signed with the Cubs in 1959 and went to the camp for prospects that year, and that's when I first met Billy. I was 19 years old, and he was 20. That was the camp in which the great Rogers Hornsby predicted we would both play in the major leagues, and he was right on.

Billy and I were teammates in San Antonio that season, and Billy was called up late in the season and got in 18 games. I got to Chicago for the second half of the 1960 season and played in 95 games, and again Billy was a late call-up and got in 12 games. The following season, 1961, we were both regulars, and we remained teammates until I went to the White Sox in 1974.

1. BILLY WILLIAMS

2. HANK SAUER

3. MOISES ALOU

4. GARY MATTHEWS

5. RIGGS STEPHENSON

Billy and I hold a record: the most games played together as teammates in major league history.

I have never seen a better left-handed hitter than Billy Williams. I can say that because I batted behind him my whole career with the Cubs, and I had

Billy and I hold the major league record for games played together as teammates (about 15 years' worth), and I couldn't dream of a better guy—or ballplayer—to have played alongside for so long. *Photo courtesy of MLB Photos/Getty Images.*

the best seat in the house watching him hit—only a few feet away in the on-deck circle. Billy was so quick, so relaxed. He could turn on a ball as well as anybody. Take Bob Gibson, who could throw the ball past most hitters; Gibby had problems with Billy. A lot of pitchers had problems with Billy Williams. Billy was just a great all-around ballplayer. And he had a great attitude.

Billy is in the Hall of Fame, and he belongs there, but I have to wonder why it took six years for him to get elected. Look at his numbers. He had almost 3,000 hits (2,711), almost 500 home runs (426), 1,475 RBIs, and a lifetime batting average of .290. He batted over .300 five times, hit more than 30 home runs five times, and drove in more than 100 runs three times. He made the All-Star team six times, was Rookie of the Year in 1961, and won a batting title in 1972. He should have been MVP that year, too, but he finished second to Johnny Bench.

Billy Williams never had it easy. Think about being a 20-year-old black kid from Whistler, Alabama, in 1959, playing in San Antonio, Texas. I can't even imagine what that must have been like. I remember on one trip to Victoria, Texas, Billy couldn't go to the same hotel as the rest of the team. I didn't understand that stuff at the time. I was a kid myself, and where I came from, Seattle, Washington, there wasn't that kind of prejudice. I thought, "What are they doing?"

What he's been through in his life is amazing. Ernie Banks didn't have to go through what Billy went through. Ernie went right from the Kansas City Monarchs in the Negro Leagues to the big leagues. Billy had some tough times. He had to play in the minor leagues in Southern towns at a time when blacks had to sit in the back of the bus, they couldn't eat in the same restaurants as whites, and they couldn't stay in the same hotels as whites.

It got to him, and one time he left the team and went home. The Cubs sent Buck O'Neill to go get him and bring him back. Billy just wanted to spend three or four days at home to clear his head. He did, and then he came back and had a whale of a year. But he needed to get away for a few days.

To go through what he went through and still become such a great player is to Billy's credit, and it shows the kind of man he is. Billy was, and is, just a beautiful person.

*R*usty Staub came to the major leagues with the Houston Colt .45s—later the Astros—in 1963, a wide-eyed rookie of 19 somewhat in awe of his surroundings. He batted against Sandy Koufax, Bob Gibson, Ferguson Jenkins, and Juan Marichal, and from his position at first base, he stared down line drives off the bat of Eddie Mathews, Willie Stargell, Willie McCovey, and Billy Williams.

"When those powerful left-handed hitters came to bat," said Staub, "I would go to the mound and tell the pitcher, 'If you throw this guy a change-up, I'm going to kill you.'

"Billy Williams was that kind of hitter. He hit line drives all over the place, and he was a great hitter in the clutch. He hit the ball as hard as anybody, and he hit line drives that would get to you in a hurry."

Staub's career closely paralleled Williams'. When Staub arrived in 1963, Williams had played two full seasons with the Cubs and had established himself as one of the National League's most reliable hitters. They would remain rivals for the next 11 seasons—Williams with the Cubs, Staub with Houston, Montreal, and the New York Mets—until Williams was traded to Oakland after the 1974 season.

Williams played 18 major league seasons, Staub 23, and amazingly, they finished their careers just five hits apart—Williams with 2,711, Staub with 2,716.

"As a fielder, he was adequate," said Staub. "I can't remember any great plays he made against us, but I can't remember him messing up any plays, either. He didn't have a great arm. He had a left fielder's arm. But as a hitter, he was one of the best.

"He'd get 200 hits, or close, every year, and he'd always hit in the .290–.310 range. I don't know why it took him six years to be elected to the Hall of Fame, but, then, I'm not surprised at anything that committee does, and that's about all I want to say on that subject."

Hank Sauer (left) poses in 1953 with new teammate Ralph Kiner, whom he'd tied for the league lead in homers the year before with 37. *Photo courtesy of Bettmann/CORBIS.*

How could someone who looked so mean be as nice a guy as **Hank Sauer** was? It proves that looks can be deceiving.

When you think of Hank Sauer, you picture a big, strong, tough-looking guy with this leathery face who was typical of the sluggers of his day—slow afoot and considered a poor fielder. But he could hit. Boy could he hit!

He won over the Wrigley Field faithful immediately by hitting 11 home runs in his first full month as a Cub, and in his first five full seasons in Chicago, he averaged 30 homers a season. In 1952, he tied Ralph Kiner for the league lead in home runs with 37, led the league in RBIs with 121, and was

Moises Alou shows all of the characteristics that made his father, Felipe, an All-Star when he was in the big leagues. His power numbers, however, are even more impressive than his dad's. *Photo courtesy of AP/Wide World Photos.*

voted the National League's Most Valuable Player even though he played for a fifth-place team.

A broken finger caused Hank to miss 44 games in 1953, and he hit only 19 homers. But he came back to hit 41 home runs in 1954 in an era when 40 homers usually put you at or near the top of the league. If he played today, Hank probably would be a 60-, maybe even a 70-home-run guy.

And talk about clutch! In his younger days, Moises Alou was as good a clutch hitter as there was. He's a guy I would want at bat when the game was on the line.

The interesting thing about Sauer is that he didn't reach the major leagues to stay until the Cincinnati Reds made him their regular left fielder in 1948. Hank was 31 at the time, and he hit 35 home runs (fourth best in the league) and drove in 97 runs. But when he got off to a poor start the following year, the Reds traded him to the Cubs for Harry Walker and Peanuts Lowrey, and Sauer became a force and a fan favorite in Chicago with his booming home runs.

Sauer also set a major league record by becoming the first player to twice hit three home runs in a game off the same pitcher. He did it against Curt Simmons of the Phillies in 1950, and two years later, he got Simmons again when he hit three solo home runs and the Cubs beat the Phillies, 3–0.

75

I played against **Moises Alou**'s dad, Felipe, and if you didn't know they were father and son, you'd have guessed they were related. That's how much alike they are. They're two of a kind. It's as if Moises is a clone of Felipe.

Not that it should be surprising, but the way Moises stands at the plate is exactly the way his father stood. They're almost identical. Not only do they hit alike, they both are good outfielders, have great arms, and get rid of the ball quickly. And talk about clutch! In his younger days, Moises was as good a clutch hitter as there was. He's a guy I would want at bat when the game was on the line. Just like his dad. And he's a good guy in the clubhouse, also like his father. Felipe is one of the best managers in the game, and, as you might figure, he passed his baseball intelligence on to his son.

The Alous are a baseball family. Felipe's brothers, Moises' uncles, Matty and Jesus also were good major league players, although not quite as good as Felipe and Moises. It's one of the great trivia answers in baseball that the three Alou brothers—Matty, Jesus, and Felipe—all played in the same outfield for the Giants at one time and in one game batted one, two, three in their batting order.

It's not unusual to see second-generation major leaguers come along with so much baseball savvy. Look at the Boones, the Bells, the Bondses, and the Matthewses.

To complete the picture of Felipe and Moises, they're probably going to end up with very similar career numbers in every category. Felipe, one of the first stars to come out of the Dominican Republic, played 17 years in the big leagues. Moises completed his 13th year in 2004, although he missed two full seasons with injuries. Felipe had a little more than 2,000 hits. Moises is over 1,700. They're pretty close in doubles, triples, and stolen bases as well.

Moises has one edge over his father. His power numbers are better, which reflects how the game has changed over the past three decades. With a few more years left, Moises already has more home runs, runs batted in, strikeouts, and walks than his father, and when his career is over, his record will be even more impressive than Felipe's.

"Sarge" earned his nickname by being a tough, disciplined leader, much like a marine drill sergeant. *Photo courtesy of MLB Photos/Getty Images.*

Gary Matthews, "Sarge," is another guy I would take with me in my foxhole. His nickname tells it all about him. He was a leader. Think of a marine drill sergeant—tough, demanding (on himself and others), competitive, aggressive.

Sarge speaks his mind. He's a guy who knows what he's talking about. He played the game the way it should be played, and he understands the game as well as anybody. I've always admired him. I admired the way he played the game. He didn't just walk out there and swing the bat and field the ball; he knew how to play the game. He was daring and mean on the bases—taking the extra base, sliding hard into second to break up double plays. Who wouldn't want a guy like that on his team? And he understands hitting—he's the Cubs hitting coach now.

Sarge came into the game hitting and running hard—he was the National League Rookie of the Year for the Giants in 1973—and he never slowed down a minute until he retired after the 1987 season.

When the Cubs got him, Matthews was coming to the end of an outstanding 16-year major league career. His best days were behind him, but he still had enough left to make an impact and to make an impression on his younger teammates. His veteran leadership helped the Cubs win a division title in 1984, when he batted .291, drove in 81 runs, led the league with 103 walks, and scored 101 runs.

Sarge's career batting average was a respectable .281, and he was remarkably consistent. In his first 12 seasons in the big leagues, he never batted above .304 and never below .279; he hit fewer than 10 home runs once and more than 20 once. That's consistency.

Riggs Stephenson may be the most underrated hitter in Cubs history. Maybe the most underrated hitter in baseball history. Here's a man who had a lifetime batting average of .336 for 14 seasons and hardly anybody remembers him. I had never even heard of him until somebody told me about him and I looked up his record. I was impressed.

There are several reasons why Stephenson was underrated:

- With the Cubs, Stephenson was overshadowed by his outfield partners: Hack Wilson in center field and Kiki Cuyler in right, both Hall of Famers. Together, they formed one of the greatest outfields of all

Stephenson (top row, fourth from left) was vastly underrated during his career, partly because he played in an outfield that also included Hall of Famers Hack Wilson and Kiki Cuyler. *Photo courtesy of AP/Wide World Photos.*

time—the only outfield in National League history in which all three members drove in 100 runs in a season, 1929.

- Stephenson was a poor outfielder with a very weak throwing arm, the result of a shoulder injury he sustained while playing football at the University of Alabama. He was originally signed as a second baseman but was shifted to the outfield because of his poor arm.
- He wasn't a big home-run hitter—only 63 in 14 seasons with a high of 17 in 1929.
- He never led the league in hitting despite averages of .344 in 1927, .362 in 1929, and .367 in 1930 (batting averages were much higher in those days).

But instead of emphasizing the negatives, we should accentuate the positives. This is a man who led the National League with 47 doubles in 1927 and who batted .319 or better in the 12 seasons in which he played at least 65 games.

Statistical Summaries

All statistics are for player's Cubs career only.

HITTING

G = Games

H = Hits

HR = Home runs

RBI = Runs batted in

SB = Stolen bases

BA = Batting average

Left Fielder	Years	G	H	HR	RBI	SB	BA
Billy Williams *Missed only 10 games between 1962 and 1971*	1959–74	2,213	2,510	392	1,353	86	.296
Hank Sauer *Had 31 multihomer games during his career*	1949–55	862	852	198	587	6	.269
Moises Alou *Hit home runs in three consecutive games three times in 2004*	2002–04	438	467	76	258	11	.283

continued	Years	G	H	HR	RBI	SB	BA
Gary Matthews *Led NL with .410 on-base percentage in 1984*	1984–87	411	320	48	176	22	.266
Riggs Stephenson *Batted over .300 each season from 1926 to 1933*	1926–34	978	1,167	49	589	39	.336

FIELDING

PO = Putouts

A = Assists

E = Errors

DP = Double plays

TC/G = Total chances divided by games played

FA = Fielding average

Left Fielder	PO	A	E	DP	TC/G	FA
Billy Williams	3,562	143	101	24	1.8	.973
Hank Sauer	1,673	75	45	12	2.2	.975
Moises Alou	646	17	16	4	2.2	.983
Gary Matthews	482	19	23	3	1.6	.956
Riggs Stephenson	1,713	65	33	17	2.0	.982

SEVEN

Center Fielder

PERCEPTION ISN'T EVERYTHING. If it was, there's no way **Hack Wilson** would have been a center fielder, let alone the No. 1 center fielder in Cubs history, and he would not have been regarded as one of the best power hitters of his day, overshadowed by Babe Ruth but worthy of comparison with Lou Gehrig, Jimmie Foxx, Chuck Klein, and Mel Ott.

In short, Hack Wilson didn't look the part.

He stood only 5'6" tall, and his 195 pounds were anchored precariously by size 6 feet, which made it appear he could easily be toppled by a Chicago wind.

Despite his squat and stumpy physique, Wilson was a nimble outfielder who, in 1927, led the league with 400 putouts. But it was as a slugger that Wilson excelled, generating enormous power with his bulging thighs and calves, muscular blacksmith arms, and barrel chest supported by a size 18 collar. He eschewed style and grace, swinging with a ferocity that was wild and undisciplined. But when he connected, the ball traveled great distances.

1. HACK WILSON

2. ANDY PAFKO

3. RICK MONDAY

4. CY WILLIAMS

5. WILDFIRE SCHULTE

The diminutive Wilson was a power hitter of epic proportions, and his 191 RBIs in 1930 still stand as the record today. *Photo courtesy of AP/Wide World Photos.*

In 1930, he smashed 56 home runs, which stood as the National League single-season record for 68 years, until Mark McGwire broke it in 1998, and he drove in 191 runs, which still stands, more than 70 years later, as the major league record.

Lewis Robert Wilson was born on April 26, 1900, in Elmwood City, Pennsylvania, and arrived in the major leagues with the New York Giants, for whom he played in three games in 1923. After a creditable rookie season in 1924 in which Wilson hacked away for a .295 average, 10 home runs, and 57 RBIs in 107 games, he fell off to .239 and was farmed out to Toledo.

After the 1925 season, the Cubs drafted Wilson for $5,000. The Giants protested, but Commissioner Kenesaw Mountain Landis denied the protest and awarded Wilson to the Cubs, one of the few pieces of good fortune in Cubs history.

Legend has it Wilson derived his nickname either from an old-time wrestler, George Hackenschmidt, or from Hack Miller, another slugger of similar build who preceded Wilson with the Cubs.

A word here about Miller, who left Chicago the year before Wilson arrived, but who would have been included among my list of all-time Cubs if he had been able to duplicate his first two seasons in the major leagues. Miller stood 5'9" and weighed 195 pounds, so one look at Wilson by Cubs fans and it was as if they were looking at a clone of Miller, a popular figure in Chicago. The two sluggers even had similar hitting styles.

Miller never was quite the hitter Wilson was, although he had his moments. A native Chicagoan, Miller failed in early trials with the Dodgers and Red Sox before arriving in Chicago and beginning his Cubs career with a bang. He batted a robust .352, third highest in the National League in his rookie season, 1922. The following year, he was third in the league in home runs with 20, drove in 88 runs, and batted .301.

Unfortunately, Miller never again showed that kind of offensive prowess.

The son of a circus strongman, Miller was famous for his displays of raw strength and his prodigious home runs. He effortlessly brandished a 47-ounce bat and entertained fans and teammates by uprooting trees and bending iron bars with his hands, pounding spikes into wood with his fist protected only by a baseball cap, and lifting automobiles by their bumpers.

In the end, it was his physique that brought about his undoing as a baseball player. He was so muscle-bound, it handicapped him defensively and robbed him of the flexibility required for Miller to fulfill the great potential he displayed early in his career. Three years after his spectacular rookie season, Miller was gone from the major leagues.

Deprived of Miller's gargantuan exploits, Cubs fans found in Wilson a suitable replacement. He was an immediate success and an instant favorite, leading the league in home runs in each of his first three seasons in Chicago. Riggs Stephenson also joined the Cubs in 1926, also by way of the draft, and took over in left field. Two years later, the Cubs obtained Kiki Cuyler in a trade with the Pirates, completing one of the greatest outfields in baseball history—Stephenson in left, Wilson in center, Cuyler in right.

In three seasons, they combined for 201 home runs and 982 runs batted in, topped off by 1929 when they each drove in more than 100 runs (Wilson, 159; Stephenson, 110; Cuyler, 102), the only outfield in National League

83

history to do so, and each batted over .300 (Stephenson, .362; Cuyler, .360; Wilson, .345).

Wilson was never the same after his watershed 1930 season. The following year, he slumped inexplicably. His batting average dipped 95 points, from .356 to .261; his home runs fell off by 43, from 56 to 13; his RBIs dropped by 130, from 191 to 61; and over the winter he was traded to the Cardinals for Burleigh Grimes, and then to the Dodgers.

The final two years of his career were with the Dodgers and Phillies, for whom he played in 191 games, hit only 17 of his 244 career home runs, and drove in only 84 of his 1,062 runs.

Even in the end, Wilson was overshadowed by Babe Ruth. He died on November 23, 1948, just three months and seven days after Ruth, and he passed away in Baltimore, the birthplace of the mighty Babe.

When people talk about the most popular players in Cubs history, the name **Andy Pafko** always comes up. Andy is in his eighties now and living in the Chicago area, so I see him a lot at Wrigley Field. I never saw him play, but I heard so much about him as a player, and after meeting him and getting to know him, I went to the record books to check him out. What I discovered was amazing.

Not only was Pafko an outstanding center fielder with a great arm, he was also a powerful hitter and a very versatile player. His manager, Charlie Grimm, called him "Handy Andy" for his versatility.

So popular was Andy that Cubs fans were outraged when he was sent to the Dodgers in a big four-for-four trade midway through the 1951 season. The previous year, Pafko had had a career year with the Cubs—a .304 average, 92 RBIs, and 36 home runs.

Twice in his eight and a half seasons with the Cubs, Pafko drove in more than 100 runs, and one of them was in 1948 when Grimm moved him in from center field to play third base and he knocked in 101. I never knew he played third base. I found that out when I set a record for RBIs by a Cubs third baseman (107 in 1967). The record I broke was Pafko's.

When he went to the Dodgers, Pafko took over left field, and with Duke Snider in center and Carl Furillo in right, he formed what was considered the greatest outfield in Brooklyn history. That year, with the Cubs and Dodgers combined, Pafko hit 30 home runs and also became a part of one of the most historic events in baseball history.

*T*he 50-year-old black-and-white film clip is indelibly inscribed into our consciousness. The ball has left the Giants' hitter's bat, soaring far and deep toward the left-field seats. The Dodgers' left fielder, his back planted against the wall, is looking up, hoping the ball will fall from the sky into his glove. When it doesn't, when the ball scrapes off the overhang, the left fielder lowers his head in despair, his shoulders slumped in frustration and disappointment.

"The Giants win the pennant! . . . the Giants win the pennant! . . ."

It's October 3, 1951, the New York Giants versus the Brooklyn Dodgers, Game 3 of the best-of-three playoff series to determine the National League championship. The Giants' hitter is Bobby Thomson, who has just smashed the "shot heard 'round the world," the most famous home run in baseball history, a dramatic walk-off three-run shot that gave the Giants a 5–4 victory and the pennant.

The left fielder is Andy Pafko, who had come to the Dodgers on June 15 in a four-for-four trade with the Cubs, possibly the most infamous trade in Cubs history.

"Andy was a big guy in Chicago," said Thomson, "a fan favorite. Cubs fans were angry when the trade was made. He was an outstanding player for the Cubs, a good hitter, a good fielder, and a hustler. Any team would want a player like Pafko."

"Andy was an excellent player," said Ralph Branca, who threw the pitch that Thomson hit over Pafko's head. "He was a good guy, a good outfielder, and he hustled. He had been a center fielder in Chicago, and a good one, but we had Duke [Snider], so Pafko moved to left field and did a good job with us.

"I do think he tried too hard when we got him. He saw that short left-field wall in Ebbets Field, and he tried to pull everything. He tried to hit home runs, and he would hit a lot of weak grounders to the shortstop. He was successful in Chicago because he hit a lot of his home runs to center field and right center."

In 49 games with the Cubs that season, Pafko hit 12 home runs, drove in 35 runs, and batted .264, but with Brooklyn for 84 games, he hit 18 homers, drove in 58 runs, and batted .249. In that celebrated playoff series with the Giants, Pafko hit a home run in each of the first two games, and his RBI single in the eighth inning of the third game had contributed to a three-run rally that gave the Dodgers a 4–1 lead heading into the fateful ninth inning.

After the 1952 season, Pafko was traded to Milwaukee. The following year, the Giants traded Thomson to Milwaukee, and for three seasons, Pafko and Thomson, linked by their roles in baseball's most storied home run, were teammates. They were not only teammates with the Braves, but also roommates on the road.

"As a roommate, he was very serious, but easy to get along with," said Thomson.

For the three years Thomson and Pafko roomed together and played together, they never discussed Thomson's home run in the 1951 playoff. Not once.

"There was no reason to bring it up," said the supremely humble Thomson. "It happened. We both knew it happened. But that was in the past. What would be the point in reopening an old wound?"

In an ironic twist, and because it seems that what goes around comes around, Thomson would become a Cub in 1958 and spend two years in Chicago, where he enjoyed a short resurgence of his career, sort of a last hurrah. He batted .283 and .259, drove in 134 runs in the two seasons, and hit 32 home runs, but need we be reminded that, alas, none of them was a walk-off, pennant-winning home run.

Any baseball fan knows all about the so-called shot heard 'round the world, Bobby Thomson's dramatic three-run, walk-off, pennant-winning home run off Ralph Branca in the final game of a three-game playoff between the Dodgers and Giants. We've all seen the film of that historic and legendary home run. Next time you see it, take a closer look. You'll see Thomson's shot disappearing into the left-field seats in the Polo Grounds, over the head of the left fielder. That Dodgers left fielder was Andy Pafko.

Pafko remains one of
the most popular
players in Cubs history.
*Photo courtesy of
Bettmann/CORBIS.*

Rick Monday spent only 5 of his 19 major league seasons with the Cubs, the first 2 while I was still there. In that time, I came to have a great deal of respect for him. To me, Rick was a great all-around ballplayer. He could run; he could hit; he could hit with power. He was a fluid outfielder with a great arm. And he was a great teammate!

He showed the kind of person he is with that incident with the flag at Dodger Stadium in 1976. The Cubs were playing an afternoon game against the Dodgers and two men jumped onto the field carrying an American flag and were about to set it on fire. Rick dashed from center field and chased after the guys. One of them threw a can of lighter fluid at him, which just missed hitting Rick. He grabbed the flag out of the guys' hands before they could set it on fire, and for that, Rick got a lot of national attention. The next day the Illinois Legislature unanimously approved May 4 as "Rick Monday Day."

Monday, shown here sliding safely past Philadelphia catcher Tim McCarver, was a truly gifted ballplayer who could beat you with his bat, his glove, his arm, and his speed. *Photo courtesy of AP/Wide World Photos.*

That's Rick. Knowing him, I'm surprised he didn't knock the guys on their behind. Rick always was well liked in Chicago, and that act made him even more popular, not only in Chicago, but all over the country.

Rick is one of those guys that wasn't all about Rick Monday. He was always about the team.

Here's a little-known fact about Rick. He was the first player taken in the free-agent draft, in June of 1965 by the then Kansas City A's. Rick was with the A's when the team moved to Oakland and was with them when they won the AL West championship in 1971. After that season, he was traded to the Cubs for another good teammate of mine, Kenny Holtzman.

Before Hack Wilson came along, even before Babe Ruth, **Cy Williams** was the foremost slugger in major league baseball, the first National Leaguer to reach 200 home runs in his career. Unfortunately, he hit most of them as a member of the Philadelphia Phillies.

Williams had been an outstanding college sprinter and hurdler at Notre Dame and had played football under the fabled Knute Rockne, but the Cubs recognized him as a hard-hitting center fielder, signed him, and brought him directly to Chicago. He never spent a day in the minor leagues, which undoubtedly slowed his development and hastened his departure from the Cubs.

Rick is one of those guys that wasn't all about Rick Monday. He was always about the team.

After being used sparingly in his first three seasons, Williams began to come on. He finished second in the league in home runs in 1915, and his 12 homers the following season tied him for the league lead.

When his home-run production fell off to just five in 1917, the Cubs grew impatient waiting for him to reach his potential and traded him to Philadelphia for an over-the-hill, 36-year-old outfielder named Dode Paskert. Cubs fans have come to view the trade as, next to Lou Brock for Ernie Broglio, the worst in team history.

In Philly, Williams blossomed. He led or tied for the league lead in home runs three times: in 1919, in 1923 with a career-high 41 (tied with Babe Ruth for the major league lead), and in 1926.

A dead-pull left-handed hitter, the original "Williams Shift" was devised for him, almost three decades before the Indians did it for Ted Williams. In his career, Williams hit 12 inside-the-park homers and seven grand slams. When his career was winding down, he was used as a pinch-hitter deluxe, his 11 pinch-hit homers standing as the major league record until 1960.

Williams played until he was 42, leaving the game after the 1930 season with a lifetime average of .292, 251 homers, and 1,005 RBIs, and with Cubs fans wondering what might have been had he not been chased out of Chicago so hastily.

89

I'm going to invoke a little editorial license here and make as my No. 5 Cubs center fielder of all time a player who was mostly a right fielder. Hey, it's my team, I can do with it what I want.

But I think you will understand my rationale when I tell you what I learned about a guy who played for Chicago 100 years ago. His name was **Wildfire Schulte**, and I wouldn't be able to forgive myself if I omitted a guy with a name like that. Another reason is that he is one of only two players in the history of baseball who had more than 20 doubles, triples, home runs,

That's Williams on the right, posing with fellow onetime-Cub Rogers Hornsby when they were both with other clubs: Williams with the Phillies and Hornsby with the Giants. *Photo courtesy of Underwood & Underwood/CORBIS.*

Schulte (No. 4 in this team photo of the world champion 1908 squad) was the National League's top player during the 1911 season, belting four grand slams, a record at the time. *Photo courtesy of the Rucker Archive.*

CHICAGO BASE BALL CLUB OF 1908.
WORLD'S CHAMPIONS.

1—Slagle	7—Overall	13—Steinfeldt
2—Reulbach	8—Hofman	14—Howard
3—Evers	9—Fraser	15—Pfeister
4—Schulte	10—Tinker	16—Brown
5—Moran	11—Lundgren	17—Chance
6—Kling	12—Sheckard	18—Durbin

and stolen bases in the same season, and the other one was Willie Mays, who was only the greatest center fielder who ever played.

Wildfire (his real name was Frank) had 30 doubles, 21 triples, a league-leading 21 homers, and 23 stolen bases in 1911. He also led the league in RBIs with 121, batted .300, hit for the cycle, and belted four grand slams, which stood as the major league record until Mr. Cub, Ernie Banks, hit five in 1955. For all of this, Schulte was awarded a Chalmers automobile as the National League's best player, 20 years before the Baseball Writers Association began selecting the Most Valuable Player.

In the early days of baseball, just after 1900, the Cubs had some of the greatest and most colorful players in the game, and Schulte was no exception. He's probably the only player ever to get his nickname from his pet horse.

Statistical Summaries

All statistics are for player's Cubs career only.

HITTING

G = Games

H = Hits

HR = Home runs

RBI = Runs batted in

SB = Stolen bases

BA = Batting average

Center Fielder	Years	G	H	HR	RBI	SB	BA
Hack Wilson *Hit for the cycle on June 23, 1930*	1926–31	850	1,017	190	769	34	.322
Andy Pafko *Named to All-Star team four consecutive seasons from 1947 to 1950*	1943–51	960	1,048	126	584	28	.294
Rick Monday *Had eight leadoff homers in 1976*	1972–76	702	690	106	293	37	.270

continued	Years	G	H	HR	RBI	SB	BA
Cy Williams *Hit 11 pinch-hit homers during his career (2 while with Cubs)*	1912–17	539	428	34	210	38	.251
Wildfire Schulte *Hit .412 in 1910 World Series loss to Philadelphia Athletics*	1904–16	1,564	1,590	91	712	214	.261

FIELDING

PO = Putouts

A = Assists

E = Errors

DP = Double plays

TC/G = Total chances divided by games played

FA = Fielding average

Center Fielder	PO	A	E	DP	TC/G	FA
Hack Wilson	2,016	67	74	17	2.6	.966
Andy Pafko	1,899	83	29	17	2.7	.986
Rick Monday	1,480	35	26	9	2.4	.983
Cy Williams	1,106	53	35	6	2.4	.971
Wildfire Schulte	2,359	178	89	37	1.7	.966

EIGHT

Right Fielder

THE EVOLUTION OF **Sammy Sosa** as one of the game's great hitters is among the most remarkable stories in baseball history. When he came to the Cubs from the White Sox in 1992, Sammy held the bat high and had to drop his hands down to hit. He hit home runs, but he didn't hit for much of an average, and he struck out a lot.

Then, to his credit, on his own he dropped his bat down and shortened his step, a slide step, and he became not only a home-run hitter but a .300 hitter as well. He took the ball to all fields with power. To me, he became a hitter that understood hitting as a man that hits home runs.

The transformation was phenomenal. Starting in 1995, Sosa hit at least 36 home runs and drove in more than 100 runs for nine straight years, and in 1998 he really blossomed into a star. That was the year of the great home-

1. SAMMY SOSA

2. ANDRE DAWSON

3. BILL "SWISH" NICHOLSON

4. HAZEN SHIRLEY "KIKI" CUYLER

5. MIKE "KING" KELLY

run race with Mark McGwire. Sammy hit 66, which would have been the major league record except that McGwire hit 70 that year.

In the four-year period from 1998 to 2001, Sammy hit 243 homers, drove in 589 runs, and also hit over .300 three times. He's going to end up with well over 600 home runs, maybe even reach 700, and he's going to be in the Hall of Fame. That's a slam dunk.

When he was younger, Sammy could run. Twice he stole more than 30 bases. And he was a very good defensive outfielder with an excellent arm. He made some great catches in right field. People have criticized him because he missed a couple of balls, but I don't criticize a player for making physical errors. Everybody makes mistakes. I criticize mental mistakes. I criticize a player if he doesn't try. And Sammy tries all the time. He's older, and he's not as good defensively as he was in his younger days, but he plays every day, unless he's hurt. He's a guy who loves to be in there every day, and he goes and gets the ball as well as anybody.

I love his flair. He's a bit theatrical, but I like that about him, and the fans love that about him. He has personality. He's a very nice guy who sometimes doesn't think about what he's saying, and it comes out the wrong way and that hurts him. But it's not malicious, and it's not intentional. You have to remember in his country, the Dominican Republic, he's bigger than the president. He's an idol there.

Take the bat-corking incident in 2003. When I heard about it, it let all the air out of me. The timing was bad, and so was Sosa's luck. They had the TV camera on the bat lying on the ground. It was as if he split the bat and dropped it in front of the umpire. How often do you see a bat break right in half? It rarely happens, but it happened to Sammy, and it hurt him at the time, but no longer. People forget very quickly, and they forgive. Sammy is so well loved in Chicago, nobody holds that against him. He's hit more than 600 home runs, and not all of them were hit with a corked bat. That incident is not going to keep him out of the Hall of Fame.

Rookie of the Year, 2,774 hits, 438 home runs, 1,581 runs batted in, 314 stolen bases, eight Gold Gloves, an MVP, an eight-time All-Star. Why isn't this man in the Hall of Fame?

I'm talking about **Andre Dawson**, "the Hawk," who played 6 of his 21 seasons with the Cubs and who I can't believe never got more than 50 percent of the vote for the Hall of Fame.

The Hawk was a great player, a ballplayer that could do it all. And fearless. Four times he led the league in getting hit by a pitch. And he's not in the Hall of Fame? I just don't understand it.

Sosa, shown here hitting his 61st home run during the great home-run race of 1998, will finish his career with the greatest power numbers in the Cubs' long history. *Photo courtesy of AP/Wide World Photos.*

Three years before, he had had his own Most Valuable Player season, and now Ryne Sandberg had a front-row seat as he watched another—what he described as "one of the greatest seasons I have ever witnessed."

Andre Dawson was no novice when he joined the Cubs in 1987. He had been a star for a decade in Montreal, Rookie of the Year in 1977, a three-time All-Star, a six-time Gold Glove winner, and twice second in the MVP voting. Three times he had batted over .300. Once he had driven in 100 runs. And he had belted 225 home runs in a 10-year period.

But he had never had a season like this.

Plagued with knee problems that he attributed to Montreal's artificial surface and determined to play on grass, Dawson, "the Hawk," had negotiated a free-agent contract with the Cubs. Boldly, and confident in his ability, he told the Cubs he would sign an "open" contract. "Just fill in the numbers you want to pay me," he said.

The Cubs filled in a salary of $500,000, less than half what he had made in Montreal the year before, plus incentives.

"He showed the Cubs he really wanted to play for them," said Sandberg.

What the Cubs got for their money was one of baseball's great bargains: a .287 average, a league-leading 49 home runs and 137 RBIs, and a Most Valuable Player, the first time the award has ever gone to a player on a last-place team.

"Dawson was one of the best teammates I ever played with," said Sandberg. "He's a class person, and he had a great work ethic. I appreciated the way he went about playing the game on an everyday basis, and the season he had was incredible.

"Because of the problems he had with his knees, what he had to do every day to go out and play was unbelievable. He put in a lot of effort and hard work in the weight room and the training room."

After six outstanding seasons with the Cubs, Dawson again became a free agent. He played two years with the Red Sox and finished out his career with two seasons with the Florida Marlins, for whom he is currently employed as a special assistant to the president. He travels with the team, gets into uniform, works with the hitters and outfielders, and waits for the call to come that tells him he has been elected to the Hall of Fame.

"In my book he's a Hall of Famer," said Sandberg. "He was one of the outstanding outfielders in his era, a player who combined power and speed."

Andre Dawson and Ryne Sandberg were teammates more than a decade ago. Maybe one day soon they'll be reunited, in Cooperstown.

Dawson came up with the Montreal Expos, was the National League Rookie of the Year in 1977, and had 10 terrific years in Montreal. But playing on artificial turf in Olympic Stadium took its toll on his knees. When he became a free agent after the 1986 season, Hawk was determined to get away from artificial turf. He made up his mind that he would sign with a team that played on grass. He had the courage of his convictions to accept a contract with the Cubs for a base salary of $500,000, far below his value and less than half what he made in Montreal.

Dawson wound up having his best years in Chicago. Natural grass and day baseball seemed to energize him. He also was going from one of the worst hitters' ballparks to one of the best. In 1987, his first season with the Cubs, Hawk led the league in home runs with 47 and RBIs with 137 and was the first player from a last-place team ever to be voted the Most Valuable Player.

In his six years with the Cubs, Dawson hit 174 homers and drove in 587 runs before opting for free agency a second time and signing with the Boston Red Sox.

Bill "Swish" Nicholson is a legendary figure in Cubs baseball for two reasons: his big, booming home runs and that colorful nickname. He picked up the nickname in Brooklyn from fans of the Dodgers who pinned it on him as a sign of derision . . . and respect. Nicholson had a big, powerful swing that often resulted in prodigious home runs, but even more often in spectacular strikeouts.

When he stepped into the batter's box, Nicholson would pump his bat several times as he waited for the pitcher to deliver the ball. With every pump, the Brooklyn fans would chant, "Swish . . . Swish . . . Swish . . ." and the name stuck.

Dawson's career seemed to be rejuvenated when he came to the Cubs in 1987, and his first year with the team remains one of the greatest seasons by a Cub. *Photo courtesy of AP/Wide World Photos.*

Originally signed by the Philadelphia Athletics, Nicholson struggled early in his career and was sent to Chattanooga in the Southern League. There, he came under the influence of Hall of Famer Kiki Cuyler, Chattanooga's manager and a former Cub. With batting tips from Cuyler, Nicholson showed remarkable improvement. He led the Southern League in home runs in two straight seasons and was purchased by the Cubs.

In Chicago, Nicholson dazzled the fans with his power, and his titanic home runs became the stuff of legend. He once drove a ball that just missed hitting the Wrigley Field scoreboard, and in a doubleheader on July 23, 1944, against the New York Giants in the Polo Grounds, he hit four consecutive home runs. The next time he came to bat, with the bases loaded and the Giants leading, 12–9, in the seventh inning, Giants manager Mel Ott ordered Swish intentionally walked.

In his first full season with the Cubs, 1940, Nicholson endeared himself to Cubs fans forever by hitting 25 home runs, second in the National League. He hit 20 or more home runs in each of his first five years with the Cubs.

When World War II came along and many of baseball's biggest stars went off to war, Nicholson was nearing 30, too old for the military. He remained with the Cubs and thrived in the talent-starved major leagues. He won consecutive home-run and RBI championships in 1943 and 1944 with a combined 62 homers and 250 RBIs. His production slipped the next two years, but he had a brief resurgence in 1947 when he belted 26 home runs but also struck out a league-leading 83 times, both totals considered high for that

Nicholson's monster home runs made him a fan favorite at Wrigley Field during the forties. *Photo courtesy of AP/Wide World Photos.*

time. Today, it's not unusual for a slugger to have 26 homers and 83 strikeouts by the All-Star break.

Cubs fans were up in arms when the popular Nicholson was traded to the Phillies after the 1948 season. But in Philadelphia, his eyesight began to fail and he was diagnosed with diabetes, and Nicholson's production declined rapidly. Nonetheless, Swish Nicholson remains one of the most beloved and most talked-about players in Cubs history.

Hazen Shirley "Kiki" Cuyler didn't come to Chicago to become a star. He brought his star with him from Pittsburgh where, in only four seasons, he established himself as one of the best players in baseball, a consistent .300 hitter, a lethal base-stealing threat, and a Hall of Famer in the making.

His trade by the Pirates to the Cubs after the 1927 season for a couple of journeymen, infielder Sparky Adams and outfielder Pete Scott, is considered one of the worst in baseball history (from the Pirates' standpoint) or one of

After coming over to the Cubs from Pittsburgh in a one-sided deal, Cuyler became a fan favorite at Wrigley Field and helped lead Chicago to pennants in 1929 and 1932. *Photo courtesy of AP/Wide World Photos.*

the best (from the Cubs' perspective) and was a mystery, and a shock, to Pirates fans.

Cuyler had burst on the scene with a bang in Pittsburgh. In his first three full seasons, he had batted .354, .357, and .321; had led the league in runs in 1925 and 1926, in triples in 1925, and in stolen bases in 1926; and was considered the heir apparent to teammate Max Carey as the National League's best base stealer. When an aging Carey was sold to Brooklyn late in the 1926 season, it was assumed that Cuyler was being primed as his replacement.

Donie Bush replaced Bill McKechnie as Pirates manager in 1927, and his grand scheme was to team Cuyler with Paul "Big Poison" Waner and Waner's brother, Lloyd "Little Poison," to give the Bucs one of the fastest and most potent outfields in the history of the game. Bush's plan also called for Cuyler to move from the third spot in the batting order to the second spot vacated by Carey.

Cuyler rebelled. In his mind, he wasn't a Punch-and-Judy, two-hole slap-hitter like Carey. He was a free swinger who took his cuts from his heels and could drive the ball out of the park. In three seasons, he had hit 34 home runs, while Carey had hit only 12.

Cuyler's reluctance to make the switch in batting positions, and the fact that he had won a salary dispute against Pirates owner Barney Dreyfuss before the season, made him persona non grata in Pittsburgh. He was benched late in the season, held out of the World Series against the Yankees, and traded to Chicago as soon as the opportunity presented itself to the Pirates.

It didn't take long for Cuyler to dispel suspicions that he was no longer the player he once was, or to become a fan favorite in Chicago. With the great slugger Hack Wilson already in place in center field and the outstanding batter Riggs Stephenson settled in left, Cuyler was the missing piece in a championship puzzle for the Cubs. Instead of Pittsburgh having the National League's best outfield, that distinction now belonged to the Cubs.

Cuyler led the league in stolen bases in his first three seasons as a Cub, and after batting a mediocre .285 in 1928, he strung together averages of .360, .355, and .330. He helped the Cubs improve from fourth place to third in 1928, and he helped them win pennants in 1929 and 1932.

Cuyler, who attended West Point before signing to play professional baseball, earned his famous, and euphonious, nickname (it's pronounced "Cuy-Cuy" not "Kee-Kee") while playing for Nashville in the Southern

103

Association. He had been called "Cuy" since high school. In Nashville, when a fly ball was lofted into short right field, fans heard the shortstop call for the right fielder to take the ball. He would shout "Cuy," and the second baseman would echo "Cuy." Soon fans, and the writers in the press box, were referring to the Nashville right fielder as "Cuy-Cuy," and the nickname caught on.

Kelly (second row, second from right), shown here with his 1880 teammates, was baseball's first matinee idol. I guess he'd compare to Derek Jeter by today's standards. *Photo courtesy of the Rucker Archive.*

In an 18-year major league career, Cuyler hit over .300 10 times (five with the Cubs), led the league in stolen bases four times (three with the Cubs), and had a lifetime batting average of .321. He was elected to the Hall of Fame posthumously in 1968, 18 years after his death.

Mike "King" Kelly might have been baseball's first superstar. If he wasn't the greatest player of the 19ᵗʰ century, he certainly was the most color- ful and the most recognizable—a dashing figure on and off the field with his flowing handlebar mustache (a sign of the times), his matinee idol good looks, his Adonis physique, his stylish and meticulously tailored wardrobe, and his flamboy- ant style of play, all of which led to his election to the Baseball Hall of Fame in 1945.

On the field, Mike Kelly was a daring and reckless base runner who once stole six bases in one game and who stole at least 50 bases in four straight seasons with a high of 84 for Boston in 1887. He did it all with a flair that aroused the passion of fans who cheered him on with "Slide, Kelly, Slide," a chant that would be turned into a popular song of the time.

To put things in modern terms, Kelly might have been the Derek Jeter of his day, the idol of millions. He got his nick- name because he was called "the king of baseball." His handsome Irish face adorned billboards across the country hailing him as America's best-dressed man, and he supplemented his income in the off-season by appearing on stages across the land.

On the field, he was a daring and reckless base runner who once stole 6 bases in one game and who stole at least 50 bases in four straight seasons with a high of 84 for Boston in 1887. He did it all with a flair that aroused the pas- sion of fans who cheered him on with "Slide, Kelly, Slide," a chant that would be turned into a popular song of the time.

When the White Stockings sold Kelly to Boston for the unheard-of sum of $10,000, Chicago's fans were so distraught, they boycotted the team except when Boston played there.

All of this would have been meaningless, of course, if Kelly had not been such an outstanding player. He played every position on the field, batted over .300 eight times, led the National League in hitting twice, and had a lifetime average of .308 for 16 seasons.

After he retired from baseball, Kelly ran a successful saloon in New York. In 1894, he was traveling to Boston to appear at the Palace Theater when he died of pneumonia. He was 36.

105

Statistical Summaries

All statistics are for player's Cubs career only.

HITTING

G = Games
H = Hits
HR = Home runs
RBI = Runs batted in
SB = Stolen bases
BA = Batting average

Right Fielder	Years	G	H	HR	RBI	SB	BA
Sammy Sosa *Only player to have three 60-home-run seasons*	1992–2004	1,811	1,985	545	1,414	181	.284
Andre Dawson *Received record five intentional walks in one game on May 22, 1990*	1987–92	867	929	174	587	57	.285
Bill Nicholson *Led NL in home runs, RBIs, runs scored, and total bases in 1944*	1939–48	1,349	1,323	205	833	26	.272

continued	Years	G	H	HR	RBI	SB	BA
Kiki Cuyler *Led NL in stolen bases three consecutive seasons from 1928 to 1930*	1928–35	949	1,199	79	602	161	.325
King Kelly *Played on five pennant winners in seven seasons with Chicago*	1880–86	681	899	33	480	53	.316

FIELDING

PO = Putouts

A = Assists

E = Errors

DP = Double plays

TC/G = Total chances divided by games played

FA = Fielding average

Right Fielder	PO	A	E	DP	TC/G	FA
Sammy Sosa	3,749	120	102	24	2.2	.974
Andre Dawson	1,481	51	20	10	1.9	.987
Bill Nicholson	2,627	107	64	19	2.2	.977
Kiki Cuyler	2,055	94	55	25	2.4	.975
King Kelly	511	206	185	15	2.0	.795

NINE

Right-Handed Pitcher

W HEN I WAS A PLAYER, I never liked being around pitchers, not even my own teammates. In my day, you didn't speak to pitchers. You didn't want them to know your personality. Remember, there was no free agency back then. You could get a phone call and just like that you're gone, and a pitcher who was your teammate and your friend was now the enemy.

In those days, pitchers pitched inside, so if you got chummy with some guy and then you got traded, the first thing he did was put one under your chin and suddenly you're not chummy anymore. So I tried not to be too friendly with pitchers.

Ferguson Jenkins was the exception. He was one of the few pitchers I loved being around. Still do. Everybody loves Fergie. "Fly"—that was his nickname—was a clown. He would see a couple of guys talking in the clubhouse, and he'd get in there and do something silly like tickle your ear.

1. FERGUSON JENKINS

2. MORDECAI "THREE-FINGER" BROWN

3. GREG MADDUX

4. KERRY WOOD

5. RICK SUTCLIFFE

As a pitcher, he was one of the best. He's in the Hall of Fame, and deservedly so. Fergie was a horse. He took the ball every fourth or fifth day, never missed a turn, and ate up innings. And every time he went out you

Jenkins, a reliever when he first came to the Cubs, is the only pitcher in the Hall of Fame with more than 3,000 strikeouts and fewer than 1,000 walks. *Photo courtesy of AP/Wide World Photos.*

always knew you had a chance to win, and you also knew he was usually going to finish what he started.

He just missed winning 300 games (he finished with 284 wins), but he completed almost 50 percent of his starts (594 starts, 267 complete games), and he's the only pitcher in the Hall of Fame with more than 3,000 strikeouts (3,192) and fewer than 1,000 walks (997). Five times he pitched more than 300 innings in a season.

Fergie never had arm problems. He had a fluid delivery and was very deceptive. He threw in the 90s, could pitch inside, and had a great breaking ball and a great change-up. And great control. He'd hit the corners low and away with consistency. He could throw it into a paper cup.

When Fergie came to the Cubs from the Phillies in a trade for Larry Jackson and Bob Buhl—another great trade by the Cubs—he was a relief pitcher. One day I walked out of the clubhouse and there was Fergie warming up on the mound with our manager, Leo Durocher, standing behind him watching with his arms folded. I walked up to Skip and said, "What do you think?"

"I'm going to make this guy a starter," Leo said.

Fergie didn't want to be a starter; he wanted to stay in the bullpen, but Leo knew what he was doing. As a starter, Fergie won 20 games or more six years in a row. Think about that: six straight 20-win seasons pitching in Wrigley Field with the short outfield walls and the wind blowing out half the time. His earned run average was kind of high, and he gave up a lot of home runs, but look where he pitched. And like so many great pitchers who also gave up a lot of home runs—Robin Roberts and Catfish Hunter, for example—they usually came with nobody on base.

In that string of six straight 20-win seasons, Jenkins also struck out more than 200 batters in all but the last season and completed at least 20 games in each of the six years. Also in that six-year stretch, he set the Cubs' modern strikeout record with 236 in 1967, then upped it in each of the following three years to 260, 273, and 274.

When Fergie fell off to 14–15 in 1973, the Cubs traded him to Texas in a deal that I may have influenced. Believing I was near the end of my career, the Cubs sent Fergie to Texas for Bill Madlock, who would take my place at third base. In his first season with Texas, Fergie rebounded with 25 wins, 29 complete games, and 225 strikeouts.

For seven years, from 1967 to 1973, Tom Seaver and Ferguson Jenkins were contemporaries and competitors, two of the elite pitchers in the National League. In that span, Seaver won 135 games and Jenkins won 141, until he was traded to the Texas Rangers.

Between them, they won 595 major league games (311 for Seaver, 284 for Jenkins), struck out 6,832 batters (3,640 for Seaver, 3,192 for Jenkins), won four Cy Young Awards (three for Seaver, one for Jenkins), and forged a relationship, although distant, based on mutual respect. Jenkins was elected to the Hall of Fame in 1991, Seaver a year later.

"To me, Ferguson Jenkins was the consummate professional," said Seaver. "He was the perfect example of someone who identified his strengths, knew what they were and how to use them. He had a great sinker and he'd get hitters to put the ball in play, but he could also strike you out. And he had exceptional control. It doesn't surprise me that he's the only pitcher in the Hall of Fame with more than 3,000 strikeouts and less than 1,000 walks."

In Seaver's and Jenkins' day, before free agency and interleague play, fraternizing with the opposition was frowned upon by the baseball establishment and eschewed by the players themselves.

"You didn't want to socialize with players from the other team," Seaver said. "You wanted to maintain a little mystery, not let your opponent know too much about you. It was part of the gamesmanship of the time, but there were a few guys I would acknowledge. Fergie was one of those guys, especially on days when neither of us was pitching. Usually, it was around the middle of the season. I'd see him and I'd get his attention and flash the number 18 with my fingers—meaning that's how many home runs I had given up. And he'd wave me off and say, 'That's nothing,' and he'd flash me a 23."

Seaver and Jenkins were never teammates, except in three All-Star Games, and they didn't have the opportunity to form a close personal bond, although they have spent time together at various functions and gatherings in Cooperstown.

"Fergie's a great guy," said Seaver. "I always found him a joy to be with. And I still do."

After spending time with the Rangers and Red Sox, Fergie came back to Chicago to finish out his career with the Cubs. In 1982, at the age of 38, he won 14 games and led the team in innings pitched.

After going 6–9 in 1983, Fergie packed it in, putting an end to a fabulous, Hall of Fame career.

A great pitcher? Yes. But more important to me, Fergie Jenkins is a wonderful, wonderful person who loves everybody. And everybody loves him.

At the turn of the 20th century, when baseball players were perceived as ne'er-do-wells, carpetbaggers, and illiterate lowlifes, along came Christy Mathewson of the New York Giants to change that perception. He was college educated, president of his class at Bucknell University, a gentleman with a reputation for clean living and sportsmanship—a perfect role model for the youth of America at a time when the sport needed positive role models.

As a pitcher, Ferguson Jenkins was one of the best. He's in the Hall of Fame, and deservedly so. Fergie was a horse. He took the ball every fourth or fifth day, never missed a turn, and ate up innings. And every time he went out you always knew you had a chance to win, and you also knew he was usually going to finish what he started.

113

And he was the dominant pitcher of his day. Mathewson won more than 30 games in a season four times, won 20 or more for 12 consecutive seasons, and finished with 373 victories in a 17-year career.

For changing the public's image of ballplayers, and for his success on the field, the game of baseball is in Mathewson's debt. But if there never had been a Christy Mathewson, **Mordecai "Three-Finger" Brown** might have been the big name in baseball at the time. He had many of the same qualities as Mathewson, without the polish acquired from a college education, and for a time he was considered the equal of Mathewson as a pitcher. And he was ahead of his time—a baseball player with a penchant for physical fitness and a bodybuilder of note whose exercise program was depicted in a national magazine, *American Monthly*, in 1914.

When the Giants met the Cubs, invariably their two aces, Mathewson and Brown, would be matched against one another, and their battles were legendary. At one point, Brown defeated Mathewson nine straight times. When they met for the last time, on September 4, 1916, each had won 12 games against the other. Mathewson, then player/manager for Cincinnati, beat Brown by the unlikely score of 10–8. It was the last game either man would pitch.

With the help of a mangled hand caused by a childhood farm accident, Brown developed one of the best curveballs in baseball and went on to a Hall of Fame career. *Photo courtesy of AP/Wide World Photos.*

When he was seven, young Mordecai's right hand was caught in a corn grinder on his uncle's farm. Most of his forefinger had to be amputated. His middle finger was left mangled and crooked. His little finger was stubbed.

It wasn't until the age of 24 that Brown turned to baseball after spending his early adult years working in a coal mine. He started as an infielder, but when he discovered that he could put an unusual spin on a baseball by releasing it off the stub of his little finger, he became a pitcher. He would turn his handicap into an advantage, winning 20 or more games for the Cubs in six consecutive seasons, from 1906 through 1911; finishing with 239 victories and a 2.06 earned run average for a 14-year career; and being elected to the Hall of Fame in 1949, the year after his death.

In addition to starting 332 games and completing 272, Brown was often used in relief and was one of the game's first outstanding relievers at a time when there were no such things as closers and starting pitchers also were used in relief. Saves were not recorded in those days, but baseball researchers, digging into the archives for old box scores, have determined that

Three-Finger was the league leader in saves for four consecutive seasons (1908–11).

Brown's enduring legacy to Cubs fans, however, was his work in the 1907 and 1908 World Series. In 1907, he pitched a 2–0, seven-hitter to complete a four-game sweep of Ty Cobb's Detroit Tigers (the first game ended in a tie).

The following year, Brown pitched two innings in relief in Game 1 of the World Series against the Tigers and was the winning pitcher when the Cubs rallied for five runs in the top of the ninth for a 10–6 victory, then came back three days later to blank Detroit, 3–0, on a four-hitter.

When Orval Overall also pitched a shutout in Game 5, the Cubs had won their second straight World Series.

I first saw **Greg Maddux** when he came to the Cubs as a 20-year-old, and I knew right then that he was something special. He was not a big guy, but he still threw hard, in the 90s, with a great change-up, a great curveball, and a lot of intelligence. He understands this game as well as anybody.

Greg is a fabulous competitor. He's old school. And he has a lot of guts. He's a guy who will pitch inside and knows how to pitch inside, and that's why he's a 300-game winner and a certain Hall of Famer.

Maddux had his greatest success with the Atlanta Braves, but he was a Cub for the first seven years of his career and won 95 games in that time, including his first 20-win season and his first Cy Young Award in 1992. After that season, he became a free agent and signed with Atlanta, where he won the Cy Young in his first three years with the Braves, giving him four consecutive Cy Young Awards.

He also won four earned run average titles and 13 Gold Gloves, the first three in Chicago.

Now, Maddux is back in Chicago where he began, and he's the first pitcher ever to win his 300th game in a Cubs uniform. He's coming close to the end of his career, but his stuff is still good and he has so much experience, he still has plenty of wins left in that arm, if he wants to keep pitching.

You normally don't see a pitcher of **Kerry Wood**'s caliber come along at such a young age with so much knowledge of the game. He has exceptional ability. He's a guy who on any given day can go out there with no-hit stuff.

Maddux won the first of four straight Cy Young Awards with the Cubs and, hopefully, will finish his career where it began. *Photo courtesy of AP/Wide World Photos.*

Wood has the tools and disposition to go down as one of the great pitchers of all time. *Photo courtesy of AP/Wide World Photos.*

117

That's how good he is. He throws 95 to 98 miles per hour and has a great curveball and change-up.

Kerry is a good all-around athlete who can help himself with his glove and his batting. He fields his position very well and he has some pop in his bat. In six seasons, he's hit seven home runs, which is rare for a pitcher and a good weapon to have going for you.

What I like most about him—and you'll hear me say this a lot—is that he hasn't forgotten where he came from. He's appreciative of everything. That's one of two qualities I respect most in a ballplayer. The other is playing the game the way it should be played. You'll hear that a lot from me as well.

Kerry is from the old school. He's a team guy and a leader as a pitcher. He'll speak up. He's not timid at all.

He's like all the great pitchers: the Gibsons, the Drysdales, the Marichals, the Carltons. When there are men in scoring position—and he might have put them there by walking a couple—he moves it up a notch and gets it done.

Kerry has had some physical problems—he's had Tommy John surgery—but if he stays healthy, there's no telling where he'll end up and how good he can be. He already has set the Cubs' record for strikeouts in a game (20 against the Astros in 1998), and his 266 strikeouts in 2003 were only 8 short of Ferguson Jenkins' team record.

118

Sutcliffe was almost unbeatable for the Cubs during their magical 1984 season, going 16–1 after coming over to the National League in a trade with Cleveland. *Photo courtesy of MLB Photos/Getty Images.*

I can't talk about Kerry Wood without mentioning another young guy, Mark Prior, who hasn't been around long enough to make my list, but who has the stuff to someday be rated among the best pitchers in Cubs history.

Mark doesn't throw as hard as Kerry does, but he has the same disposition. He respects his peers and respects the fans. Both of them do. They're both just dynamite. And both of them are very intelligent. They understand all facets of the game, and that, to me, is very important.

The only difference between Wood and Prior: Mark's command is better and Kerry's fastball is better.

Rick Sutcliffe is a very dear friend. Anybody can get along with Sut. He's a clown. He loves to have fun with everybody. He's a very intelligent and outgoing guy who's in a business he should be in: he's a baseball broadcaster for ESPN. And he's very good at it.

As a pitcher, Rick came along at the right time for the Cubs when they got him from Cleveland in June of 1984. He wound up going 16–1 for the Cubs (he had won four games for the Indians, so he was a 20-game winner for the only time in his career), won the Cy Young Award, and was a big reason they won the National League East title.

Sutcliffe was the winning pitcher when the Cubs clinched the division title and the winning pitcher in Game 1 of the National League Championship Series against San Diego when he pitched seven shutout innings (and hit a home run). And he became the center of controversy later in that series.

The Cubs had won the first two games of the best-of-five series, but they lost the third game. A lot of people thought Sutcliffe should have pitched Game 4. It was his normal day to pitch and he was ready. When you have the other team down, you don't let them up, but manager Jim Frey was saving Sutcliffe for the first game of the World Series and started Scott Sanderson instead. The Padres knocked Sanderson out in the fifth inning and came from behind to win Game 4 and tie the series at two games each.

Sutcliffe started Game 5 for the Cubs, but by then the momentum had shifted and the Padres again came from behind to beat Sut and advance to the World Series. To this day, most Cubs fans believe things would have been different if Frey had given Sutcliffe the ball for Game 4.

Statistical Summaries

All statistics are for player's Cubs career only.

PITCHING

G = Games
W = Games won
L = Games lost
PCT = Winning percentage
SHO = Shutouts
SO = Strikeouts
ERA = Earned run average

Right-Handed Pitcher	Years	G	W	L	PCT	SHO	SO	ERA
Ferguson Jenkins *Last NL righty with 30 complete games in a season (1971)*	1966–73 1982–83	401	167	132	.559	29	2,038	3.20
Mordecai Brown *Pitched 13 complete-game 1–0 victories in his career*	1904–13 1916	346	188	86	.686	48	1,043	1.80
Greg Maddux *Has won 15 or more games a record 17 straight seasons beginning in 1988*	1986–92 2004	245	111	86	.563	14	1,088	3.0

continued	Years	G	W	L	PCT	SHO	SO	ERA
Kerry Wood *Has 41 double-digit strikeout games in his career*	1998 2000–04	164	67	50	.573	5	1,209	3.63
Rick Sutcliffe *In 1984, became the first pitcher since 1945 to win 20 games in a season split between AL and NL*	1984–91	193	82	65	.558	11	909	3.74

FIELDING

PO = Putouts

A = Assists

E = Errors

DP = Double plays

TC/G = Total chances divided by games played

FA = Fielding average

Right-Handed Pitcher	PO	A	E	DP	TC/G	FA
Ferguson Jenkins	187	394	30	23	1.5	.951
Mordecai Brown	149	600	21	27	2.2	.973
Greg Maddux	209	366	17	29	2.4	.971
Kerry Wood	59	96	5	11	1.0	.969
Rick Sutcliffe	118	251	10	15	2.3	.974

TEN

Left-Handed Pitcher

I DON'T WANT YOU TO MISUNDERSTAND ME here when I say that to me, **Kenny Holtzman** was a lot like Sandy Koufax. Now, I'm not comparing Holtzman to Koufax. I'm not saying he was as good as Koufax. You can't compare anybody to Koufax. I put Sandy ahead of any pitcher I've ever faced and any pitcher I've ever seen in the major leagues.

But there were similarities between Koufax and Holtzman because Kenny could throw the ball 95 to 97 miles per hour, and he had a great curveball. Like Koufax, Holtzman could be a dominant pitcher, and he was on occasion.

One of those occasions happened to be in a game he pitched against Koufax, the only time they went head-to-head in their careers. It was September 25, 1966, Koufax' last season and Holtzman's first. Koufax would win 27 games that year; lead the league in wins, ERA, strikeouts, complete games, and shutouts; and then retire because of an arthritic elbow.

1. KENNY HOLTZMAN

2. JAMES "HIPPO" VAUGHN

3. DICK ELLSWORTH

4. LARRY FRENCH

5. JACK PFIESTER

Holtzman, a 20-year-old rookie, would win 11 games for the Cubs and lose 16, but on this day, Kenny got the better of the master. He took a no-hitter

He didn't necessarily have the career that Sandy Koufax did—no one could—but Holtzman, at times, could be as dominant as the Hall of Famer. *Photo courtesy of MLB Photos/Getty Images.*

124

into the ninth inning and ended up winning the game, 2–1, handing Koufax his ninth loss of the season, and the last loss of his fabulous career.

Two other times, Holtzman was Koufax-like. I witnessed both of them from my position at third base. On August 19, 1969, Kenny pitched a no-hitter against the Braves in Wrigley Field. I hit a three-run homer in the first inning off Phil Niekro, and that was the only scoring in the game. We won, 3–0, and the odd thing is that Holtzman didn't strike out a single batter.

Two years later in Cincinnati, against the Reds—the Big Red Machine of Johnny Bench, Tony Perez, George Foster, and Dave Concepcion—Holtzman pitched a second no-hitter. That time he beat Gary Nolan, 1–0, on an unearned run. Holtzman scored the run himself. He led off the top of the third by reaching on an error by Perez, went to second on a ground ball, and scored on a single by my roomie, Glenn Beckert.

*B*etween them, they won 462 major league games and another 12 in playoffs and World Series. Tommy John, who won 288 games before he became a surgical procedure, and Ken Holtzman, who won 174, never played together, but they almost did, and one can only imagine what wondrous things they might have accomplished jointly had fate conspired to make them teammates.

Tommy John tells the story of what might have been: "I was a senior in high school in Terre Haute, Indiana, in 1961, and I was recruited by one college for baseball—the University of Illinois. The coach there was a man named Lee Eilbach, and he had my mom and dad and me up for a weekend. We went to see an Illinois–Ohio State basketball game, and he showed us around the campus. He said, 'If you come here, we're going to have a good ballclub, but the next year, the class of '62, we're going to be even better because we have a left-hander out of East St. Louis coming here, a kid named Ken Holtzman. From what I've seen, you two left-handers can dominate in the Big Ten.'"

Holtzman ended up going to the University of Illinois at Urbana-Champaign and then being drafted by the Cubs in the fourth round of the June 1965 free-agent draft and leaving college to sign a professional contract.

"I opted to sign with the Cleveland Indians instead of going to college," said John, "but Holtzman and I could have been teammates."

John spent two years in Cleveland, won only two games for the Indians, and was traded in 1965 to the White Sox with Tommie Agee and John Romano for Rocky Colavito and Camilo Carreon. Again, his path would cross with Holtzman's, a Cubs rookie.

"When I got to Chicago," said John, "I hooked up with Joey Amalfitano, who was a coach with the Cubs, and we shared an apartment. When the Cubs were away, the White Sox were home, and vice versa, so Joey and I rarely saw one another. Later, I traded Joey in for Sally, my wife, which might be the best trade in baseball history."

Occasionally, the two teams would be home at the same time, and because the Cubs played all their games in the day, John would go to Wrigley Field.

"I'd spend time with Joey and Yosh Kawano, the clubhouse man, and watch some of the game," said John. "That's when I first got to see Holtzman. I went out one day and the Phillies were in town. Before the game, I was talking with Dick Allen and Dick said, 'I'm 0 for 4 today.'

"I said, 'What do you mean?'

"He said, 'Holtzman is pitching and he'll throw me fastballs on the outside corner and I can't hit them. I keep swinging at them, but I can't hit them.'

"Dick Allen could turn any fastball around, but he couldn't hit Holtzman, who didn't throw exceptionally hard. I don't know how hard Holtzman threw because we didn't have radar guns in those days, but he had that funky little arm cock, and he came over the top, and he had a good, riding fastball, and Allen couldn't hit him.

"Later, when he pitched in the World Series with the Oakland Athletics and was outstanding, all Kenny threw was that riding fastball and a little fadeaway change-up. Fastball. Change-up. Boom . . . boom . . . boom. Kind of like Tom Glavine pitches today, but Holtzman had a little better fastball than Glavine."

It's a remarkable, and almost unbelievable, coincidence that these two left-handers, who came close to going to the same college, who played for two of the same major league teams, and who combined to pitch in 1,211 major league games in a combined 41 years, most of them overlapping, never were teammates and never pitched against each other. There were a few opportunites for them to do so, but it never happened.

From 1965 to 1971, both played in Chicago—Holtzman with the Cubs, John with the White Sox. There was no interleague play then.

In 1974, Holtzman's Athletics and John's Dodgers met in the World Series. Holtzman started Games 1 and 4. John did not pitch in the Series.

In 1978, Holtzman's Yankees met John's Dodgers in the World Series. John started Games 1 and 4. Holtzman did not pitch in the Series.

Holtzman left the Yankees during the 1978 season. John joined the Yankees in 1979.

Holtzman left Oakland after the 1975 season. John joined the Athletics 10 years later.

On those occasions, Holtzman showed the promise of becoming one of the best pitchers in the National League. In 1967, his second season, he was 9–0, but he spent most of the season in the military. In 1969 and 1970, he won 17 games each year. In six seasons with the Cubs, he was 74–69, and then he was traded to Oakland for Rick Monday in one of those trades that helped both teams. We needed a center fielder, and Monday turned out to be a good one. Meanwhile, Holtzman became a mainstay with that great Oakland pitching staff of Catfish Hunter, Blue Moon Odom, and Vida Blue. He won 77 games for the A's in four seasons and helped them win three straight World Series (Holtzman was 4–1 in World Series games).

During his career, Kenny picked up a reputation for being aloof. I guess he was, to the outside world, but that wasn't how his teammates saw him. To us, he was a funny guy with a good sense of humor, and very intelligent. His teammates loved him. We adored him.

I was very happy for his success because I liked Kenny and consider him one of the best teammates I ever had. He's a guy I would want with me in a foxhole any day of the week.

Later, Kenny would come back to the Cubs and spend the last year and a half of his career in Chicago, but things had changed a lot by then. I had retired, and Holtzman was at the end of his career. In 1979, his final season, he was 6–9 and showed only brief flashes of the pitcher he used to be when he shut out the Astros twice, on a three-hitter and a six-hitter.

During his career, Kenny picked up a reputation for being aloof. I guess he was, to the outside world, but that wasn't how his teammates saw him. To us, he was a funny guy with a good sense of humor, and very intelligent. His teammates loved him. We adored him.

The thing about Kenny is that he's a very private person who always went his own way. Even today, he doesn't show up for a lot of things that he's invited to. About the only place he shows up regularly is at Randy Hundley's Fantasy Camp.

When I lost my legs because of my diabetes, Kenny sat down and wrote me a beautiful letter that touched me very deeply. It's a letter I treasure, just as I treasure my friendship with him.

James "Hippo" Vaughn's place in baseball history is secure, dubious though it may be, as the losing pitcher in the greatest game ever pitched. His place in Cubs' history is secure in a more positive way.

127

Vaughn's no-hit performance on May 2, 1917, will forever endure in baseball lore—he unfortunately wound up losing the game to Cincinnati's Fred Toney in the only double no-hitter in history. *Photo courtesy of the National Baseball Library Archive.*

Vaughn's 151 career victories place him eighth on the Cubs' all-time list, first among left-handers. He also ranks in the Cubs' top 10 career list in earned run average (2.33), games started (270), complete games (177), shutouts (35), innings pitched (2,216), strikeouts (1,138), and opponents' batting average (.241).

In nine seasons with the Cubs, Vaughn, a native Chicagoan, won 20 games or more five times, including three consecutive years, 1917, 1918, and 1919. In 1918, he led the National League in wins (22), ERA (1.74), starts (33), innings (190⅓), strikeouts (148), and shutouts (8). If there had been a Cy Young Award presented at the time, Vaughn would have been the easy winner over his more famous contemporaries, Burleigh Grimes, Rube Marquard, and Art Nehf.

For all his accomplishments, Vaughn's signature moment came in a game he lost. It happened on May 2 in Chicago's Weeghman Park, now Wrigley Field. The Cubs met the Cincinnati Reds with Vaughn drawing as his opponent right-hander Fred Toney, a bear of a man at 6'6", two inches taller than Vaughn, and a former Cub. Later that season, Toney would pitch and win both games of a doubleheader against Pittsburgh.

Toney and Vaughn would battle all season for the runner-up position to Philadelphia's Grover Cleveland Alexander for the most wins in the National League, and their duel on May 2 was a microcosm of that season-long battle. Through nine innings, neither pitcher had allowed a hit.

Both pressed on into the tenth. Vaughn retired Gus Getz, the first batter for the Reds in the top of the tenth, but Larry Kopf followed with a single. It was the first hit of the game, and it would be the game's only hit. After Greasy Neale flied to center fielder Cy Williams for the second out, Williams muffed Hal Chase's fly ball for an error, putting runners on second and third.

The next hitter was the legendary Carlisle Indian and Olympic champion Jim Thorpe, who tapped a ball along the third-base line. Vaughn sprang from the mound, picked up the ball, and, realizing he had no chance to get the speedy Thorpe at first, fired home. The throw caught catcher Art Wilson by surprise, hitting him in the chest protector, and Kopf scored the game's only run.

Toney completed his no-hitter in the bottom of the tenth, and Vaughn was the hard-luck loser of baseball's only double no-hit game, the greatest two-man pitching performance in baseball history. At the time, both men were credited with pitching a no-hitter; however, in 1991, baseball amended the standard for a no-hitter. It decreed that a pitcher would not be credited with a no-hitter even if he pitched nine hitless innings but allowed a hit in a later inning. As a result, poor Hippo's name is not included on any list of no-hitters, except as a footnote to Toney's gem.

Ellsworth was one of those guys who always had the potential to come out and be virtually unhittable, as he nearly was on this day in 1963, when he held the Phillies to one bunt single in a 2–0 win. *Photo courtesy of AP/Wide World Photos.*

Toney finished the season with 24 wins, one more than Vaughn, but Hippo came back the following year with his finest season and pitched three complete games in the 1918 World Series against the Red Sox, losing to Babe Ruth in Game 1, 1–0, losing to Carl Mays in Game 3, 2–1, and beating Bullet Joe Bush in Game 5, 3–0. That left the Cubs down, three games to two.

The Red Sox won Game 6 and took the World Series. They would wait 86 years before winning another World Series in 2004.

When I joined the Cubs midway through the 1960 season, my first roommate was **Dick Ellsworth**. We were both just a couple of 20-year-old kids, but he had been up briefly in 1958, and he started the 1960 season with the Cubs. So, he was the "veteran," and I was the "rookie," and he showed me the ropes even though I am 26 days older than Dick.

I often wondered why Ellsworth didn't have a better career than he did. He had a great sinkerball and a very good breaking ball, and he was very smart and knowledgeable about pitching and hitters.

In 1962, Dick lost 20 games, but the next year he won 22. How does that happen? It's Ellsworth the 22-game winner that caused me to rate him as the third-best left-hander in Cubs history.

After the 1966 season, Dick was traded to the Phillies, and then he bounced around to the Red Sox and Indians and finished up with the Brewers. He had a few good years (he won 16 games for Boston in 1968) but never again attained the heights he reached when he won 22 games (three fewer than Sandy Koufax and Juan Marichal, one less than Warren Spahn and Jim Maloney) in 1963.

In his relatively brief time in Chicago (six and a half seasons, from 1935 to 1941), **Larry French** was a workhorse for the Cubs, doubling as a starter and reliever. He had come to the Cubs from the Pirates in 1935 and was a vital part of their record 21-game winning streak that lifted the Cubs to the National League pennant. French won 5 games in that 21-game stretch.

His durability is attested to by the fact that in the decade of the 1930s, only the great Hall of Famer Carl Hubbell pitched more innings than French, who logged 2,481. For seven straight years, he appeared in 40 games.

In his first two years with the Cubs, French led the National League in shutouts, and he finished his career with 40 shutouts, 21 of them in Chicago,

That's French on the left, and Fred Lindstrom on the right, with manager Charlie Grimm in the middle after the two former Pirates joined the Cubs for spring training in 1935. *Photo courtesy of Bettmann/CORBIS.*

which places him ninth on the team's all-time list in that category. In his first three years as a Cub, he won 51 games, and he finished his career with 197 wins (he would have topped 200 had World War II not come along), 95 of them as a Cub.

French was sold to the Dodgers during their stretch run to a pennant in 1941. He appeared in two games in the 1941 World Series against the Yankees, including the memorable Game 4. French was the second of four pitchers in the game, painfully remembered in Brooklyn as the one in which the Yankees, trailing by a run, rallied for four in the top of the ninth when catcher Mickey Owen failed to catch a pitch thrown by Hugh Casey at which Tommy Henrich swung and missed for what should have been a game-ending strikeout.

That's Pfiester in the top row, second from the left, on the 1906 Cubs squad that lost the World Series to their crosstown rivals, the White Sox. *Photo courtesy of AP/Wide World Photos.*

French ended his career with a flourish, leading the National League in winning percentage with a 15–4 record for the 1942 Dodgers. He joined the navy in 1943 and turned it into a second career, retiring from active duty in 1969 with the rank of captain.

No. 5 on my all-time list of Cubs left-handers is a toss-up between two pitchers from long ago, Jake Weimer, who was with them from 1903 to 1905, and **Jack Pfiester**, who was a Cub from 1906 to 1911.

Both were 20-game winners, Pfiester in 1906, Weimer in 1903 and 1904, but I give the nod to Pfiester, based on longevity and because he won 70 games as a Cub, 11 more than Weimer.

Statistical Summaries

All statistics are for player's Cubs career only.

PITCHING

G = Games

W = Games won

L = Games lost

PCT = Winning percentage

SHO = Shutouts

SO = Strikeouts

ERA = Earned run average

Left-Handed Pitcher	Years	G	W	L	PCT	SHO	SO	ERA
Ken Holtzman *Threw three consecutive shutouts in 1968*	1965–71 1978–79	237	80	81	.497	15	988	3.76
Hippo Vaughn *Credited with stealing home on August 9, 1919*	1913–21	305	151	105	.590	35	1,138	2.33
Dick Ellsworth *Last Cubs lefty to win 20 games in a season (22 in 1963)*	1958 1960–66	254	84	110	.433	6	905	3.70

continued	Years	G	W	L	PCT	SHO	SO	ERA
Larry French *Pitched two scoreless innings in NL's 4–0 victory in 1940 All-Star Game*	1935–41	272	95	84	.531	21	642	3.54
Jack Pfiester *Led NL with 1.15 ERA in 1907*	1906–11	143	70	40	.636	17	482	1.85

FIELDING

PO = Putouts

A = Assists

E = Errors

DP = Double plays

TC/G = Total chances divided by games played

FA = Fielding average

Left-Handed Pitcher	PO	A	E	DP	TC/G	FA
Ken Holtzman	52	212	14	11	1.4	.958
Hippo Vaughn	73	571	58	14	2.3	.917
Dick Ellsworth	82	340	21	22	1.7	.953
Larry French	72	324	16	18	1.5	.961
Jack Pfiester	57	269	22	5	2.0	.925

ELEVEN

Relief Pitcher

I'M NOT GOING TO BE THE FIRST GUY to tell you that relief pitching is different today than it was in my day, or that the role of the so-called closer has changed dramatically.

I have all the respect in the world for Mariano Rivera and Eric Gagne, but don't tell me they're any better than the stoppers of the seventies and eighties like Rollie Fingers, Goose Gossage, **Bruce Sutter**, and Lee Smith. Imagine if Sutter were pitching today, when all he'd have to do would be come in to pitch the ninth inning, nobody on base, and often with a three-run lead. If that were the case, Sutter would have had 40, 50, even 60 saves every year instead of the 37, 28, 25, 36, and 45 he had that still led the league.

1. BRUCE SUTTER

2. LEE SMITH

3. RANDY MYERS

4. PHIL REGAN

5. DON ELSTON

That's why Sutter belongs in the Hall of Fame. He's not there, and if he never gets there it's because times have changed. It's a different era and today's relievers are putting up saves numbers that dwarf Sutter's. But that doesn't—or it shouldn't—mean today's relievers are better than Sutter.

Sutter's numbers look minuscule compared to the number of saves guys are putting up today, but the closer's role has changed dramatically over the past 30 years and you could still make a case for his being the best ever. *Photo courtesy of AP/Wide World Photos.*

To give you an idea of how relief pitching has changed, when Sutter had 45 saves for the Cardinals in 1984, he pitched in 71 games and had 122⅔ innings, or almost 2 innings an appearance. In 2003, Gagne had 55 saves and pitched 82⅓ innings in 77 games, or just about an inning and a third per outing. Now look at Mike Marshall in 1974. He appeared in 106 games and pitched 208 innings, or 2 innings per appearance, and he saved only 21 games. But he won 15.

I missed playing with Sutter by a couple of years. He was signed by the Cubs in 1971 but didn't get to Chicago until 1976, two years after I retired. Bruce almost never made it to Chicago. In 1973, he had arm surgery that threatened to end his career before it really got started. But he rebounded and, with the help of Cubs pitching coach Mike Roarke, developed the split-fingered fastball, a slight variation of what used to be called the forkball.

Sutter was a pioneer of the pitch that became a staple in almost every pitcher's repertoire in the nineties and beyond. That pitch—and he was a master at throwing it—turned Sutter into a great—and I mean GREAT—relief pitcher.

*P*robably the greatest single change in baseball on the field over the past four or five decades has been the emergence of the relief pitcher, his rise to prominence, and the dramatic evolution of his role. In the past, the reliever usually was a pitcher who was not good enough to crack the starting rotation or a veteran who no longer had the stuff or the stamina to pitch nine innings.

Today, a reliever, or closer, is one of an elite group, a cult hero, a celebrity of rock star proportions. He is the cowboy who rides in on the white horse to save the damsel in distress in Hollywood Westerns, the fireman who pulls a child out of a burning building, the superhero who rids Gotham of the nefarious villain. And he is paid commensurate with the great stars of the game.

For that, the likes of Mariano Rivera, Eric Gagne, Troy Percival, Trevor Hoffman, Joe Nathan, Francisco Cordero, Armando Benitez, Keith Foulke, and Jason Isringhausen owe a debt of gratitude to their forebears—relievers who blazed the trail in the sixties, seventies, and eighties, such as Hoyt Wilhelm, Rollie Fingers, Dennis Eckersley, Goose Gossage, and Bruce Sutter.

In a brilliant 25-year career, Jim Kaat has known both sides of the pitcher's mound, as a starter and a reliever. He won 283 major league games, 24 of them in relief. Had he not conceded to time and team loyalty and remained a starter, he might have won 300 games and thereby been elected to the Hall of Fame. By going to the bullpen, Kaat came to a greater appreciation of the relievers of his day and beyond. He places Sutter, his teammate for three years with the Cardinals, at, or near, the top of the list.

"In 1981," said Kaat, "we were involved in a tight race in the National League East. We went to Shea Stadium for a big series with the Mets. We battled back from a four-run deficit and took a 6–5 lead into the bottom of the ninth. Sutter went in, so we figured game's over. He was that dominant.

"Sutter got the first two guys out, and then Frank Taveras hit an 0–2 splitter, broke his bat, and hit a bloop single. Then Mookie Wilson took an 0–2 splitter over the fence and we lost the game, 7–6. It was a shocking loss because Sutter almost never lost a game like that.

"Sutter called me 'old timer,' because I was the oldest guy on the team. He was the 'Amishman' because of his beard. We left Shea and boarded a plane for Chicago, and I said to him, 'Well, Amishman, what are you going to do tonight?'

"'I'm going to have a couple of cold beers,' he said, 'and hope we have a one-run lead in the ninth inning tomorrow.'

"The next day, Joaquin Andujar pitched against the Cubs, and we had a 2–0 lead going into the eighth. Sutter pitched two innings [Editor's note: Sutter actually pitched only one inning in that game]—in those days closers often pitched two, even three and sometimes four innings—and got right back on track.

"What made Sutter so great was his demeanor and his determination. He wouldn't get too high after he saved a game, and he wouldn't get too low on the rare occasions when he blew a save. He had the perfect temperament for a closer. And, of course, he was a pioneer in throwing the split-fingered fastball, and he was devastating. For a five-year period, from 1980 to 1984, the 'Amishman' may have been the most dominant reliever of all time."

In 1977, Sutter had his breakout year. He saved 31 games—that doesn't sound like a lot by today's standards until you realize that Fingers led the majors with 35 saves—and also won 7 games and had an earned run average of 1.35. Two years later, Bruce led the majors with 37 saves and won the Cy Young Award.

Although I never hit against Sutter (I'm grateful for that) and I never played behind him, I followed him closely when he was a Cub. He was amazing—and at times unhittable.

He'd come into games in the seventh, eighth, or ninth inning, and he always got the job done.

Sutter had the perfect demeanor for a closer. He never got too high after a good game or too low when he blew a save. When he went to the mound, the impression you got was that he was in control, and more often than not he was.

After he led the league in saves again in 1980, the Cubs traded Sutter to their archrivals, the Cardinals. I'm not sure why. Maybe they feared Bruce was slipping a little—he went from 37 saves to 28—or maybe they felt the

Smith, Sutter's successor in the Cubs bullpen, was big, hard-throwing, and just plain nasty. He may have been the most intimidating reliever of all time. *Photo courtesy of MLB Photos/Getty Images.*

need to acquire a third baseman (Ken Reitz) and a slugger (Leon "Bull" Durham).

As it turned out, Sutter had his best years with the Cardinals, leading the league in saves three more times and compiling his best record in 1984, when he saved 45 games. That season got him a big six-year, eight-figure free-agent contract from the Braves, but he came up with shoulder problems and saved only 40 games in three years and was forced to retire.

Lee Smith may have been the most intimidating reliever ever, thanks to his impressive size. A hitter would get into the batter's box and look out at the mound at this huge guy on the hill, 6'6" tall, anywhere from 240 to 270 pounds, and with a menacing glare on his face.

Even good hitters would see a guy like this on the mound and think, "Oh, boy!" He was a presence. He looked as if he threw hard . . . and he did, in the high 90s. He looked mean . . . and he was. He threw hard and he pitched inside. And he came up with a great slider.

Hitters would go up there, look at this mountain of a man on the mound, and figure he was just going to rear back and throw the ball as hard as he could. So they would sit on Smith's fastball, and Lee would throw them that slider, and they had no chance.

Hitters would go up there, look at this mountain of a man on the mound, and figure he was just going to rear back and throw the ball as hard as he could. So they would sit on his fastball, and Lee would throw them that slider, and they had no chance.

When I speculated on the reasons the Cubs traded Bruce Sutter to the Cardinals, what I failed to mention as possibly part of the equation was that Smith was coming along and the Cubs figured they had Sutter's replacement. Lee took over the closer's role when Sutter left and saved 31 games in 1981, 37 in 1982, and 41 in 1983.

Smith spent eight seasons with the Cubs and racked up 180 saves, still the team record. After the 1988 season, the Cubs traded Smith to the Red Sox. It's rare that a closer can remain effective for more than eight seasons, and that was probably part of the Cubs' thinking in trading Lee. To his credit, he stayed around for 10 more years with the Cardinals, Yankees, Orioles, Angels, Reds, and Expos—an 18-year career, which is remarkable for a relief pitcher.

Smith's career was remarkable not only for its length but also for what he accomplished. When he retired after the 1997 season, he was baseball's all-time saves leader with 478 despite never having more than 47 saves in any one season because of the way closers were used in his day.

Randy Myers came to the Cubs as a free agent in 1993 and in his first year saved 53 games, which still stands as the team single-season record for saves. For a couple of years, I would put Randy in a category with Sutter, Smith, and the other great relievers.

Basically, Myers was a two-pitch pitcher—a fastball and a slider—which is all you really need as a closer. He had the ability to reach back and get a little more when he needed it, and occasionally he would reach 100 miles per hour with his fastball.

Myers was, in many ways, the prototypical closer. He had a fastball that hovered around 100 mph and a very good slider, and he was a little on the goofy side. *Photo courtesy of Getty Images.*

That's Regan, whom they used to call "the Vulture" for his late-inning relief victories, taking a throw from Ernie Banks in spring training 1971. *Photo courtesy of Bettmann/CORBIS.*

Randy was a free spirit who never took himself seriously and often would make humorous, disparaging remarks about his own ability. Let's face it, he was a little goofy, and that's another quality you often find in great relief pitchers.

Phil Regan was my guy—the relief pitcher I played behind for a good part of my career—and I have the greatest respect for him. You're not going to see a lot of gaudy numbers next to his name. He didn't compile a great number of saves—only 92 in a 13-year career with four teams. But remember, he pitched in what can be described as the "Dark Ages" where relievers are concerned.

When he pitched for the Dodgers, they nicknamed Phil "the Vulture," because he would come in late in a game and shut down the other team, and the Dodgers would score late and he'd pick up the win (he was 14–1 with a league-leading 21 saves for the Dodgers' 1966 National League champions).

I faced him, and he was tough. He'd come in and eat you up, just like a vulture. He didn't have the greatest stuff, but it was good enough, and he could spot the ball where he wanted to. It was hard to pick up his ball. He had a good sinker and slider that would jump at you.

He also had the best demeanor of any relief pitcher I have known. I never saw a more determined or a gutsier pitcher. And he was very intelligent. It seems he's been around the game forever, as a scout and a coach, and he even managed one season with the Orioles.

When I joined the Cubs in Pittsburgh as a 20-year-old midway through the 1960 season, that first night they put me in a room with **Don Elston**, who

Elston was the jack-of-all-trades on the Cubs pitching staffs of the fifties and sixties. Long relief, set-up man, closer—he could do it all, and he did it all well. *Photo courtesy of AP/Wide World Photos.*

had been around about 10 years by then. Although my first full-time room-mate was Dick Elsworth, Don Elston was the first guy I roomed with in the big leagues. It was for only one night, but you never forget your first big-league game, your first big-league hit, or your first big-league roommate.

Don was very accommodating to me, and I've never forgotten that. As I said before, in those days rookies were often not treated as equals by veter-ans. You had to prove yourself first. But Don couldn't have been nicer.

Elston wasn't a big guy—about 6' tall, 165 pounds—but he knew how to pitch. He was your basic sinker, slider, curveball, change-up type pitcher, and he was a guy who could pitch every day. In 1958, he pitched in 69 games, a Cubs record at the time. The following season, he and Bill Henry both pitched in a league-leading 65 games for the Cubs.

The Cubs weren't a very good team in those days, so Elston's record is not particularly impressive, but believe me, the man could pitch, and he could handle any job—long man, set-up man, closer. Elston did it all. In those days, he *was* the Cubs' bullpen.

Statistical Summaries

All statistics are for player's Cubs career only.

PITCHING

G = Games

W = Games won

L = Games lost

PCT = Winning percentage

SHO = Shutouts

SO = Strikeouts

ERA = Earned run average

Relief Pitcher	Years	G	W	L	PCT	SHO	SO	ERA
Bruce Sutter *Finished four consecutive All-Star Games from 1978 to 1981, winning one and saving two*	1976–80	300	32	30	.516	133	494	2.39
Lee Smith *Led league in saves four times and was runner-up four times*	1980–87	458	40	51	.440	180	644	2.92

continued	Years	G	W	L	PCT	SHO	SO	ERA
Randy Myers *His 53 saves in 1993 is the single-season record for a lefty*	1993–95	168	4	11	.267	112	177	3.52
Phil Regan *Led NL with 25 saves his first season with Cubs in 1968*	1968–72	246	32	26	.552	60	177	3.44
Don Elston *Picked up the save in the first of two All-Star Games played in 1959*	1953 1957–64	449	49	54	.476	63	518	3.70

FIELDING

PO = Putouts

A = Assists

E = Errors

DP = Double plays

TC/G = Total chances divided by games played

FA = Fielding average

Relief Pitcher	PO	A	E	DP	TC/G	FA
Bruce Sutter	44	61	4	1	0.4	.963
Lee Smith	33	73	1	7	0.2	.991
Randy Myers	3	19	1	0	0.1	.957
Phil Regan	29	79	4	6	0.5	.964
Don Elston	45	128	11	12	0.4	.940

TWELVE

Manager

Y OU MIGHT HAVE HEARD STORIES about **Leo Durocher** and me—that we fought with each other and that we had a strong dislike for each other. I can tell you now that those stories are not true . . . at least they're not entirely true.

Sure, Durocher and I had our disagreements. I'm not going to say we didn't. Leo was brutally honest. He wouldn't let you get too close to him, and he didn't believe in trying to win friends by soft-pedaling things. He always said what was on his mind, even if it hurt. I liked that. What I didn't like was having a conversation with a manager who wasn't honest enough to look you in the eye when he talked to you. That wasn't Leo's way. You might not like what he said, but deep inside you knew what he was saying was true, and you had to accept it.

1. LEO DUROCHER

2. DON ZIMMER

3. CAP ANSON

4. DUSTY BAKER

5. CHARLIE GRIMM

The problem I had with him was over something he said. I'm not going to tell you what it was—it would serve no purpose now—but I went after him. I had my hands around his neck. Leo wasn't a very big guy, and he was in his sixties at the time, but he showed no fear. He stood right up to me. He

Leo and I had our disagreements, but that doesn't change the fact that he was the best manager I ever had. *Photo courtesy of MLB Photos/Getty Images.*

was tough, and I respected that. I came to respect him a great deal, and I loved playing for him. He was the best manager I ever had.

I first got to know Durocher when he was the third-base coach for the Dodgers. He had a reputation as a fierce umpire baiter and bench-jockey, but he was always very nice to me. I'd be at my position, and he'd be in the coach's box, and we'd engage in small talk. One day, he said to me, "The Dodgers are interested in you."

I was in my second year with the Cubs, and I have to admit I was flattered. But I also was a little disturbed. I started thinking, "Am I going to get traded?"

Then in 1966, Durocher became our manager and we could see things begin to change. Not at first. We finished last in 1966, but the next year we moved up to third, and by 1969 we were pennant contenders.

Leo "the Lip" Durocher, one of the most flamboyant, colorful, and contro-versial characters in baseball history, was many things to many people.

To his defenders, he was intelligent, fiercely competitive, ahead of his time, tough, daring, suave, debonair, quick-witted, and a brilliant field strategist.

To his detractors, he was crude, irascible, cantankerous, egomaniacal, abra-sive, brash, unyielding, confrontational, profane, tactless, and a scoundrel.

Renowned as a relentless umpire baiter and bench-jockey, he nonethe-less was acclaimed as a managerial genius that made teams better and was always one step ahead of his counterpart in the opposing dugout.

Legend has it that as a young player with the Yankees he was accused of stealing Babe Ruth's watch. In 1945, he was indicted for assaulting a fan under the stands. And there were rumors that he consorted with known mobsters and racketeers. Perhaps they were more than just rumors because in 1947, Commissioner Happy Chandler suspended Durocher for associating with known gamblers.

Durocher enjoyed the company of Hollywood types with a rough edge and shady past like Frank Sinatra and actor George Raft, and it was said that he was often sycophantic in their presence.

Despite his dark side, Durocher is revered for his baseball knowledge. Ralph Branca has known both Durochers: the brilliant managerial strategist who was a mentor and a motivator, and the unyielding, bench-jockeying, umpire-baiting manager in the opposing dugout.

Branca was a mere lad of 18 when Durocher brought him to Brooklyn in 1944. The following year, Branca started 15 games for the Dodgers, com-pleted 7, and won 5. Durocher planned to include Branca in his starting rota-tion for the 1946 season, but the pitcher was undermined by one of Durocher's coaches and dropped from the rotation until late in the season.

Desperate for starting pitching, Durocher overruled his coach and handed the ball to Branca in the heat of a pennant race with the Cardinals. The man-ager's faith in the 20-year-old was rewarded when Branca shut out the Car-dinals, 5–0, on September 14, and then came back four days later and blanked the Pirates, 3–0, in the second game of a doubleheader.

When the Dodgers and Cardinals finished the regular season tied, necessitating the first playoff in National League history, Durocher chose the young right-hander to pitch the opening game of the best-of-three series. Branca failed to make it to the third inning, but Durocher's confidence in him, Branca believes, was one of the main factors that contributed to his greatest success as a pitcher.

When the 1947 season started, Durocher was under suspension and replaced by Burt Shotton, who included Branca in his starting rotation. At the age of 21, Branca started 36 games for the Dodgers; completed 15; won 21, one behind the league leader Ewell Blackwell; and had an earned run average of 2.67 to help the Dodgers win the pennant. He was the Dodgers' starting pitcher in the opening game of the World Series against the Yankees. Branca lost that game but came back in relief to win Game 6.

"Durocher was serving out his suspension that year," Branca recalled, "but I have always felt that by starting me in those two games in the pennant race in September, and then starting me in the first game of the playoffs, that boosted my confidence and helped me win 21 games in 1947.

"I thought Leo was a very, very good manager. I remember sitting there listening to him during a game, and he'd be figuring out moves he would make a few innings later. 'If I bring in so-and-so, they'll counter by bringing in so-and-so.' I was just a kid, and I was amazed that he was charting all his moves in advance. And this was long before they had computers. He did what he thought was right, and he constantly outmanaged the other guy."

Four years after Branca's 21-win season for the Dodgers, Durocher was the enemy. He had returned to the Dodgers in 1948 after serving out his one-year suspension, but in a shocking midseason move, he leaped across the Harlem River to replace Mel Ott as manager of the hated New York Giants. Dr. Jekyll had been transformed to Mr. Hyde, and on one memorable October afternoon in New York's Polo Grounds, Durocher was in the third-base coach's box when Branca tried to throw a fastball past Bobby Thomson and failed.

"If Leo had one fault as a manager," Branca said, "it was that he believed in jabbing everybody with a needle, and you can't manage every player the same way. Some guys you have to jab, some you have to stroke.

"In later years, I thought Leo got a little too Hollywood. He liked to hang out with big stars, and that affected him a little.

"In 1969, when he managed the Cubs and they blew that big lead and lost to the Mets, people blamed Leo. They said the game had passed him by and he couldn't relate to the players anymore. I don't believe that. I think that was just a case of the Mets catching lightning in a bottle. They had that great pitching under Gil Hodges, and they just caught fire. The Cubs didn't lose the pennant that year. The Mets won it."

When we learned that Leo was going to be our manager, all the players were excited. I mean, he's Leo Durocher, a legend. The Gashouse Gang. He won pennants. All of a sudden, we had respect.

The first thing he did when he came to us was hold a meeting where he said, "I am the boss on the field. I am the manager, not the coach. Don't go over my head. I make all the decisions." He was very direct. He said, "You guys bunt when you should hit-and-run, you hit-and-run when you should bunt. We're going to change all that. We're going to play fundamental baseball."

Leo didn't have to look at the lineup card to know who was coming up the next inning and the inning after that. He was always a step ahead of everybody. He was very competitive and very aggressive. When he put on the uniform, nobody in the other uniform was his friend. If one of our hitters got knocked down, Leo didn't have to tell our pitchers anything. They knew he expected them to protect their teammates.

The players loved him and respected him. He was quite a character. He was a fancy dresser, and he liked to hang out with stars. We'd go to Los Angeles, and there'd always be some celebrity in the clubhouse. Don Rickles would come in. Frank Sinatra would come in. One night, Leo invited Glenn Beckert, Joe Pepitone, and me to go out to dinner with Frank Sinatra at Sinatra's country club. That was a night I'll never forget, and Leo Durocher is a man I'll never forget.

Don Zimmer is another guy I have a great deal of respect for. I never played for him, but I played with him, and I observed him as a manager with the Cubs and liked his style. Zim did things his way. He didn't manage out of a book; he managed with his gut. He did a lot of unorthodox things, like hit-and-run with the bases loaded, and he got the Cubs into the playoffs in 1989.

Nobody ever accused Zim of doing everything by the book, but his unorthodox style paid off with a division title in 1989. *Photo courtesy of AP/Wide World Photos.*

154

Popeye was the first veteran player to pay any attention to me. When I first came up, veterans had very little to do with rookies. There were only 400 players in the major leagues at the time, and you might be taking some veteran's job, so you had to prove yourself before they'd even talk to you.

When I came up to the Cubs during the 1960 season, Zimmer was playing third base, but they moved him to second to make room for me. He was a seven-year veteran, but he never showed any resentment toward me. In fact, he was very supportive and even outspoken in his support.

In 1961, the Cubs were experimenting with their college of coaches. Instead of a manager, they had six coaches, and they would rotate them as "head coach," so every two weeks we had a different coach running the team. Zim was, and still is, a guy who speaks his mind, and he got on the radio with Lou Boudreau and began knocking the coaching system, calling it ridiculous. "You're going to ruin two of the best young players in the organization, Billy Williams and Ron Santo," he said.

I had been with the Cubs only a few weeks, and we were in Milwaukee and Zim came up to me and said, "What are you doing tonight?" I said I had no plans, and he invited me to go out to dinner with him and Dick Gernert. As I said, it was unusual for a veteran player to even talk to a rookie, let alone invite him to dinner.

We went to a restaurant called Fazio's, where a lot of the players hung out, and Zim said to me, "What are you drinking?"

I had never had a drink of alcohol in my life. I still don't drink. So I told Zim that I didn't drink, and he said, "Have a gin and tonic. It will taste like soda."

So I ordered a gin and tonic. It was a hot night, and the drink was refreshing. I ended up having three or four gin and tonics. I was feeling fine until I got up to go to the men's room and went right to my knees.

Popeye introduced me to something else. I had never been to a racetrack, and Zim loved to go to the track and still does. So one day he took me to the track in St. Louis. Zim did all the handicapping, told me what horses to bet, and I left there with about $1,000 in my pocket.

How can you not love a guy like that?

Young Cubs fans of today—even old ones—are going to find it hard to believe that there was a time when their beloved Cubbies were the dominant team in baseball, a powerhouse and a dynasty, winning five championships in seven years, three of them in a row.

Of course that was in baseball's Dark Ages, before 1900, and the team wasn't even called the Cubs in those days; they were known as the White Stockings

The man who led Chicago to all those titles was **Cap Anson**, a player/manager. He guided the team for 19 seasons, from 1879 through 1897, and won 1,296 games, earning a reputation as a leader of men, a tireless ambassador for the game, an innovator, and a showman. He also was demanding, explosive, combative, a cruel bench-jockey, a vicious umpire baiter, and, from all accounts, a racist.

Anson once pulled his team off the field prior to an exhibition game against Newark of the International League when he noticed the Newark

FEW AND CHOSEN

He wasn't exactly a warm, likable figure, but it's hard to argue against the managerial success of Cap Anson around the turn of the century. *Photo courtesy of MLB Photos/Getty Images.*

catcher, Fleet Walker, was African American. And he is said to have been a driving force in banning blacks from playing in the major leagues—an unwritten code that lasted until 1947, 25 years after Anson's death.

His strictness with his players, his temper, his fierce competitiveness, and his explosiveness were legendary in his day. He was ruthless in his remarks directed at opposing players from the Chicago bench and in his attacks on umpires. He laid down strict training rules for his players, who often rebelled against them. And it's said Anson was not unwilling to enforce his rules or challenge umpires' rulings with his fists.

Despite all that, Anson made great contributions to the game of baseball and was regarded as one of the game's pioneers, a man at the forefront of forging the game's early popularity. Some of his innovations are still in use today. He was one of the earliest managers to encourage his players to steal bases, to implement the hit-and-run play, to rotate his pitchers (in earlier days, before Anson, one man frequently pitched every one of his team's games), to employ the use of platoons, and to recognize the value of spring training.

Anson was instrumental in spreading the gospel of baseball to foreign lands. He took part in a baseball tour to England in 1874 and a world tour in

1888–89 and is credited with helping to raise the caliber of players with his integrity and principles and with spreading the popularity of the game, thereby securing his place in baseball history.

Anson's place in Cubs history is secured in the fact that when he left Chicago after the 1897 season, in tribute to how closely he was linked with them, the team was briefly known as the "Orphans."

It didn't take long for **Dusty Baker** to win the respect of Cubs fans, Cubs players, and me. Dusty is an outstanding manager. For one thing, he's won over 1,000 games, so that tells you a lot about him as a manager. He's not only

Dusty is unquestionably a players' manager, which I think is important in today's age. It's one reason I think he'll bring a World Series championship to Chicago. *Photo courtesy of AP/Wide World Photos.*

a good baseball man and very intelligent; the best thing about him is how he handles players.

No manager can keep all 25 players happy, but Dusty comes closer to doing it than any manager I've ever seen. He's a player's manager. One-on-one with a player, he's the best. Everybody loves playing for him. He's a manager who's going to utilize all 25 players on his roster and keep them all involved.

Dusty Baker is going to be the Cubs' manager for a long time, and he's going to bring the Cubs their first World Series championship in almost 100 years, and he's going to do it soon, I hope.

Dusty Baker is going to be the Cubs' manager for a long time, and he's going to bring the Cubs their first World Series championship in almost 100 years, and he's going to do it soon, I hope.

158

Although my professional relationship with **Charlie Grimm** was brief and unpleasant, I came to admire this man for all he accomplished as a player, a manager, and a general ambassador of baseball. When I got to know him in later years, after he had retired to Arizona, I found him to be a wonderful man, full of life, fun-loving, and all baseball; one of the great characters in the history of the game; and a beloved ex-Cub.

You may remember me telling you that I accused Charlie of lying to me in the spring of 1960. I had been invited to spring training as a nonroster player, and Charlie, 64 years old at the time, had just returned for his third tour as manager of the Cubs, and he told me that if I had a good exhibition series against the Dodgers in the next-to-last weekend of spring training, I would make the ballclub. I had a very good series against the Dodgers and figured I had the team made. But then John Holland, the general manager, said they were sending me back to the minor leagues.

I blamed Grimm. I accused him of lying to me, and I stormed out of the meeting. I realize now that it was not Grimm's fault. He and Holland were doing what they thought was best for the team, and for me. But I was too young, too inexperienced, too emotional, and too hurt to have seen it back then. In retrospect, everything worked out just fine.

When I finally got to the Cubs in June of 1960, Grimm was no longer the manager, so I never played for him. He was fired after 17 games and replaced by Lou Boudreau, who had been in the broadcast booth. They simply changed jobs. Grimm went upstairs to the booth, and Boudreau came down on the field and was my first manager.

Grimm was one of the most colorful and beloved figures in baseball for decades and a fiercely loyal Chicago Cub. In fact, following his death in 1983, his ashes were scattered over Wrigley Field. *Photo courtesy of Time Life Pictures/Getty Images.*

Through my years in Chicago, I have learned that Grimm is one of the great Cubs heroes, both as a manager and a player. Grimm broke in with Connie Mack's Athletics in 1916 but didn't become a regular until four years later with Pittsburgh. He quickly gained a reputation as the finest first baseman of his time. He would win nine fielding titles with the Pirates and later the Cubs. He also batted over .300 five times and finished with a career batting average of .290 for 20 seasons.

Maybe I'm doing Charlie a disservice by not picking him among my top five Cubs first basemen of all time, but I obviously never saw him play, and I know so little about him. And, because he played in the dead-ball era, his power numbers do not measure up to first basemen of later years.

Grimm was considered a free spirit—a guy who liked to have fun, on and off the field. That's how he got his nickname "Jolly Cholly." In Pittsburgh, he teamed with shortstop Rabbit Maranville and second baseman Cotton Tierney to form a trio of cutups the likes of which you don't see anymore.

Charlie was a left-handed banjo player, and he would often strum the thing in the clubhouse, even after Pirates losses, which didn't go over very well with the team's brass.

In those days, there was a famous vaudeville team called Gallagher and Shean. Their act consisted of songs and patter, usually ending something like this:

"Is that correct, Mr. Gallagher?"

"Yes it is, Mr. Shean."

Grimm must have been a big fan of Gallagher and Shean because he often adopted their songs and appropriated them for his own. One day, a sharp ground ball was hit to Grimm's right. He snared it just a few feet from the bag, but instead of stepping on first, he threw the ball to his second baseman, shouting, "Have we got him, Mr. Tierney?" To which Tierney replied, "Absolutely, Mr. Grimm," then threw the ball back to Grimm for the putout.

Despite his excellence on the field, Grimm's antics started to wear on Pirates management, and after the 1924 season he and Maranville were traded to the Cubs, where Grimm became firmly established as the team's first baseman. By 1932, Charlie was in his eighth season with the Cubs. When the team started slowly, manager Rogers Hornsby was fired and replaced by Grimm as player/manager. The Cubs were not responding to Hornsby, a tough taskmaster. Grimm was just the opposite: easygoing and tolerant, a players' manager.

Under Grimm's loose rein, the Cubs ran off a 14-game winning streak in September and won the pennant. Grimm led the Cubs to another pennant three years later, but in 1938, he abruptly resigned, saying he felt he could no longer relate to or control his players. Grimm moved into the broadcast booth, and Gabby Hartnett took over as manager.

In 1941, Grimm left the broadcast booth and went back down on the field as a Cubs coach. He left the Cubs to take over as manager of the Milwaukee club in the American Association, and then he returned to the Cubs as manager in 1944. A year later, he led the Cubs to another pennant and their last appearance in the World Series. Charlie was relieved as manager of the Cubs in 1949, and for the next two decades he was a baseball nomad. He worked in the Cubs' front office, left to return to the minor leagues as manager of Milwaukee, left there in 1952 to become manager of the Boston Braves, went with the Braves as their manager when they moved to Milwaukee, returned to the Cubs as manager in 1960, and was fired and went back to the broadcast booth and stayed with the Cubs for 15 years in a variety of front-office jobs until he retired in 1975.

When Charlie died in 1983, his widow asked for, and received, permission to scatter his ashes over Wrigley Field.

Statistical Summaries

All statistics are for manager's Cubs career only.

MANAGING

G = Games managed

W = Games won

L = Games lost

PCT = Winning percentage

P = Pennants

WS = World Series victories

Managers	Years	G	W	L	PCT	P	WS
Leo Durocher *Cubs finished over .500 in six of the seven seasons he managed them*	1966–72	1,065	535	526	.504	0	0
Don Zimmer *His 93 victories in 1989 is the most for the Cubs over the past 20 seasons (1985–2004)*	1988–91	524	265	258	.507	0	0

continued	Years	G	W	L	PCT	P	WS
Cap Anson *Had record .798 season winning percentage (67–17) in 1880*	1879–97	2,258	1,283	932	.579	5	0
Dusty Baker *Led Cubs to consecutive winning seasons (2003–04) for the first time in 32 years*	2003–04	324	177	147	.546	0	0
Charlie Grimm *Posted Cubs last 100-win season (100–54) in 1935*	1932–38 1944–49 1960	1,737	946	782	.547	4	0

THIRTEEN

Team

I realize I'm putting my neck squarely on the chopping block here. I know I'm going to get some disagreements, some arguments, but I'm ready for them. I *should* be ready for them. I have been having these same arguments for the past 35 years, every time I make the claim that the **1969** Cubs, *my* 1969 Cubs, were the greatest team in Cubs history.

Believe me, I know it's a hard sell to say that a team that won only 92 games, blew an 8½ game lead in mid-August, and finished eight games behind the Miracle Mets, is the best team in Cubs history, and yet there are thousands of Cubs fans old enough to remember the 1969 team who will agree with me. And there's nobody still alive who can argue for the 1906–1908 Cubs.

Maybe you had to be there in 1969—and I *was* there, right in the middle of it all. Obviously, I'm prejudiced, but I played 15 seasons in the major leagues, and the 1969 Cubs stand head and shoulders above any other team I played for, not only as players, but also as people.

That team had everything—pitching, hitting, and defense. Three players on that team—Ernie Banks, Billy Williams, and Ferguson Jenkins—made

1. 1969

2. 1906

3. 1929

4. 1945

5. 2003

Our 1969 squad had four players with 20 or more homers, including (from left) Billy, me, and Jim Hickman. *Photo courtesy of the Rucker Archive.*

the Hall of Fame, along with manager Leo Durocher. We had two guys with more than 100 runs batted in (I had 123, Banks 106) and four with more than 20 home runs (me, Ernie, Billy, and Jim Hickman, as well as Randy Hundley with 18). We had two pitchers who won 20 games (Fergie and Bill Hands, as well as Ken Holtzman, who won 17); a great reliever in Phil "the Vulture" Regan, who won 12 games and saved 17; and an infield that most people considered the best in the game at the time.

So what went wrong? I like to think that 1969 was one of the rare times that the best team did not win.

I'm not taking anything away from the Mets. They won the pennant and they deserved it. They just kind of snuck up on everybody, got hot in August, and kept rolling. Up until that season, the Mets, who came into the league in 1962, had never finished higher than ninth. They never had a winning season.

The most wins they ever had were 73. So they just took everybody by surprise in 1969.

That year the Mets were a young team. They had a bunch of strong-armed pitchers who were just beginning to blossom, including Tom Seaver in his breakout season—a 25–7 record and a 2.21 ERA—Jerry Koosman, Gary Gentry, Nolan Ryan, and Tug McGraw in the bullpen. That great pitching carried an offense that batted only .242 as a team and hit only 109 home runs. They had nobody with more than 76 RBIs, and only one player with more than 20 homers (Tommie Agee, who belted 26 batting leadoff). But they got great production from role players like Ken Boswell, Ron Swoboda, Art Shamsky, Wayne Garrett, and Ed Kranepool, and they added a big bat when they picked up Donn Clendenon on June 15. They caught fire in August and just couldn't be stopped.

Still, we had an 8½ game lead on August 19 and we should have been able to hold onto it. There was a lot of criticism leveled at our manager, Leo Durocher, because five of us played at least 151 games that season, and because the Big Three of our pitching staff—Jenkins, Hands, and Holtzman—combined for 122 starts and 872 innings. But I don't buy into it. We were young, strong athletes, in our physical prime. There was no reason we should have worn down, and I don't think we did. We just got blindsided by a team with great pitching that was on a roll.

I was the captain of that 1969 Cubs team and I would take the lineup card up to home plate before every game. Leo would hand me the lineup and I would look at it and there would be no changes. But I didn't expect any changes. We had a solid team of young veterans, proven major leaguers, good players. There was no reason to sit any of them. I never heard anybody asking out of the lineup, and I never heard anybody complain that they were tired. We went though a period where we just stopped hitting, but it had nothing to do with fatigue.

A lot was made about two games we lost to the Mets in July. We went into Shea Stadium for a three-game series leading the Mets by 5½ games, and lost the first two games—devastating losses.

In the first game, we took a 3–1 lead into the bottom of the ninth. Fergie Jenkins was pitching brilliantly. He had allowed only one hit (a home run by Kranepool in the fifth), had walked none, and struck out eight. The way Fergie was pitching looked like a sure "W," and that might have put the Mets

Ernie, looking ready to swipe a base here, was the fourth member of the 20-dinger club and the undisputed leader of the 1969 Cubs. *Photo courtesy of MLB Photos/Getty Images.*

168

away for good, right there. But they rallied for three in the bottom of the ninth and won the game, 4–3.

The next night Seaver was tremendous against us. He allowed just one hit (a single by rookie outfielder Jimmy Qualls with one out in the ninth), struck out 11, and beat us 4–0, his 14th win against only 3 losses. That cut our lead to 3½ games and some people say that's when the Mets turned things around. But I disagree. We bounced back to win the final game of that series, lost a game in Philly, and then won four straight, and we even fattened our lead to 8½ games. So those two losses to the Mets in New York weren't the turning point.

That came later, when we went to the West Coast and lost a few games while the Mets continued to win. That's when the momentum shifted to them. We weren't hitting. I remember thinking to myself before a game, "What's going to happen next?" Nobody said anything out loud, but I figured if that's what I was thinking, the other guys were thinking the same thing. When you think something bad is going to happen, that's when it usually does. Instead of being aggressive and going out and making good things happen, we were sitting back waiting for bad things to happen. And they did.

Blowing an 8½ game lead and losing the pennant to the Mets was tough to take—a bitter pill for Cubs fans, one of many they have had to endure. It still hurts all these years later and the reason it hurts is that I believed then that we were the best team in baseball in 1969. I still believe it. I always will.

All right, I'll submit peaceably and go back almost 100 years for No. 2 on my list of the greatest Cubs teams, only I'm just not certain if it should be the **1906**, 1907, or 1908 team. All three won the National League pennant. The 1907 and 1908 teams won the World Series—the last times the Cubs won the Series, by the way. The 1906 Cubs lost to the White Sox in the World Series, but those Cubs won 116 games, a record that stood for 95 years until the 2001 Seattle Mariners matched that win total. Nobody has broken that record.

Actually, the 1906 Cubs stand ahead of the 2004 Mariners. The Cubs won their 116 games in a 154-game schedule for an all-time record winning percentage of .763, while the Mariners did it in a 162-game season (how come nobody gave them an asterisk?) and had a winning percentage of .716. What's more, the 1906 Cubs played three ties (there were no lights in those days and games were suspended because of darkness) that were never made up because they were not necessary to determine a pennant winner. If they had been made up, the Cubs surely would have won at least one of those games and would hold the record all alone.

When you think about it, those three teams in 1906, 1907, and 1908 were essentially the same, with all the same players—pitchers Mordecai "Three-Finger" Brown, Jack Pfiester, Ed Reulbach, Carl Lundgren, and Orval Overall (I love that name), Johnny Kling behind the plate, Jimmy Sheckard and Wildfire Schulte in the outfield, and that famous infield of Joe Tinker, Johnny Evers, and Frank Chance.

Chance had started his career as a catcher, but had been switched to first base when Kling came along in 1902. When the Cubs finished a disappointing third in 1905, manager Frank Selee was fired late in the season and

Harry Steinfeldt (left) poses with the famed trio that helped the 1906 Cubs to a record 116 victories: the immortal Tinker-to-Evers-to-Chance. *Photo courtesy of MLB Photos/Getty Images.*

replaced by Chance as player/manager. Chance would lead the Cubs to pennants in his first three years as manager and would come to be known as "the Peerless Leader." Imagine winning 116 games and finishing 20 games ahead in the National League in your first full season as a manager!

But the season was destined to end in what would become typical Cubs disappointment. Matched with the American League champions—their crosstown rivals the Chicago White Sox—the heavily favored Cubs lost the third World Series ever played. That White Sox team was known as "the Hitless Wonders," and they lived up to their reputation by batting only .198 as a team in the Series. But they held the Cubs to a .196 batting average and won the Series in six games.

The Cubs came back strong in 1907 when they won 107 games, finished 17 games ahead of Pittsburgh, and then beat the Tigers in the World Series in five games (the first game ended in a tie).

The Cubs made it three straight pennants when they finished a game ahead of the Giants and Pirates in 1908, the year of the famous "Merkle Boner," and then won their second straight World Series from the Tigers in five games.

So, in the three years from 1906–08, the Cubs won 322 games, three National League pennants, and two World Series, making them the first dynasty in baseball's so-called post-1900 "modern" era.

Another rookie manager put his imprint on the Cubs when Joe McCarthy was brought out of the minor leagues to take over the team in 1926. McCarthy,

It was an all-Chicago World Series (imagine that!) in 1906, and the Sox ended up winning four games to two. *Photo courtesy of MLB Photos/Getty Images.*

Hall of Famer Hornsby batted .380 with 39 home runs and 149 RBIs to lead the 1929 Cubs to 98 victories and their first pennant in 11 years. *Photo courtesy of MLB Photos/Getty Images.*

who would go on to manage those great Yankees teams of the thirties and forties, showed his leadership, his influence, and his tough-mindedness, and asserted his authority almost immediately with the Cubs. He fought for—and won—the removal from the team of malcontents such as the legendary veteran and future Hall of Famer Grover Cleveland Alexander, and he convinced the Cubs to acquire outfielders Hack Wilson and Riggs Stephenson, then in the minor leagues.

McCarthy's moves produced immediate dividends, improving the team's record by 14 games and four places in the standings: he finished fourth in 1926 with a record of 82–72. Three years later, after obtaining Kiki Cuyler from Pittsburgh and the great Rogers Hornsby from the Braves, the **1929** Cubs won 98 games, finished 10½ games ahead of the Pirates, and won their first pennant in 18 years.

Fans in Philadelphia packed the roofs of row houses overlooking Shibe Park to watch the A's topple the Cubs in the 1929 World Series, four games to one. *Photo courtesy of AP/Wide World Photos.*

The Cubs outfield of Stephenson, Wilson, and Cuyler is regarded as one of the greatest, if not the greatest, in baseball history. In 1929 all three batted over .340 (Stephenson .362, Cuyler .360, Wilson .345), and drove in more than 100 runs (Wilson 159, Stephenson 110, Cuyler 102).

Hornsby, at age 33, batted .380, knocked in 149, and hit 39 homers. And Pat Malone (22), Charlie Root (19), and Guy Bush (18) combined for 59 wins and 15 saves.

Once again, however, the season ended in disappointment for the Cubs when they ran into the powerful Philadelphia Athletics in the World Series. The A's of Connie Mack, with future Hall of Famers Jimmie Foxx, Al Simmons, Mickey Cochrane, and Lefty Grove, had won 104 games in the American League. They overwhelmed the Cubs in the World Series in five games.

A year later, with the Cubs in second place and four days left in the season, McCarthy resigned as manager amid rumors that he was heading for New York, and was replaced by Hornsby. Those rumors proved true when McCarthy was named Yankees manager on October 10, 1930.

For No. 4 on my list of the greatest Cubs teams, I'm probably going to raise some eyebrows again by picking the **1945** team. The reason some may disagree is that this team won a pennant in a watered-down league when most of the game's best players were off serving their country in World War II. But this was the last Cubs team to win a pennant, and that fact cannot be ignored.

The 1945 Cubs won 98 games and beat out the Cardinals by three games. Would that have happened if there wasn't a war on? Nobody knows. But I can tell you from what I have heard and read that that was a very good team. They were managed by my old friend Charlie Grimm and led by first baseman Phil Cavarretta (who won the league batting title with a .355 average, drove in 97 runs, and was named National League Most Valuable Player), and by Andy Pafko (who batted .298 and drove in 110 runs).

The 1945 team also had Cubs favorites Bill "Swish" Nicholson and Peanuts Lowrey in the outfield and Stan Hack at third.

Hank Wyse won 22 games, Claude Passeau 17, and Paul Derringer 16, but the key to the season was a deal the Cubs made on July 27. With the Cubs in a three-way dogfight for the National League pennant with the Cardinals and the Dodgers, they purchased right-hander Hank Borowy from the Yankees for $97,000.

There was a war still on in 1945, and many of baseball's greatest players, like Joe DiMaggio, Ted Williams, Stan Musial, and Bob Feller, were missing from major league fields. But President Franklin D. Roosevelt had decreed that the game should go on even while the war was raging in Europe and Asia.

As long as there was baseball, and as long as they were keeping score, and as long as they were still awarding a pennant, somebody had to win. In the National League, that somebody was the Chicago Cubs.

The Cubs had won the pennant in 1938, but ravaged by age, they would begin a free fall the following season, a steady descent that would see them drop to fourth, fifth, and then sixth place in consecutive seasons. Eventually there was slight but steady improvement: fifth place in 1943, fourth in 1944. And by 1945, war or not, the Cubs were ready to contend.

"A lot of good players were in the war," said Andy Pafko, a center fielder on the 1945 Cubs, their last pennant winner. "Maybe the leagues were a little weak. Would we have won if every team had all their players back? That's hard to say; I know one thing, we had a good ballclub. Phil Cavarretta, Stan Hack, Bill Nicholson. Hank Wyse, Paul Derringer, and Claude Passeau on the pitching staff. And then we got Hank Borowy from the Yankees. I don't know why the Yankees let him go, but I'm glad they did. He won 11 games for us. We wouldn't have won without him."

Having won in 1945, there were high expectations that the Cubs could contend again the following season, but they slipped to third place—14 games behind the Cardinals. Perhaps it was because the Cards were reinforced by the return of Musial and Enos Slaughter, perhaps not.

"We won in 1945 because we had a lot of older players who were not eligible for the draft, and that age just caught up with us," said Pafko, one of the few members of the 1945 team who still had his best years ahead of him. He had batted .298 in 1945 and led the Cubs in RBIs with 110, fourth most in the National League. But he was no wartime warrior. He would play 14 more years after the war and have his best seasons with all the teams at full strength, topping a .300 batting average in 1947, 1948, and 1950, and driving in 101 runs in 1948 when he was asked to fill a void for the Cubs by moving to third base, hitting 36 home runs in 1950.

And then on June 15, 1951, Pafko was traded to the Brooklyn Dodgers.

"I never could figure it [the trade] out," said Pafko, now a sprightly 84. "I was brokenhearted when I got traded, and the way it happened was a shock to me. We were playing a three-game series against the Dodgers in Wrigley Field, and I remember during batting practice before the first game Don Newcombe yelled out to me, 'Hey, Pafko, you're going to be a Dodger tomorrow.' I had never even heard any rumors.

"After the second game of the series, I went home and my wife was making dinner when the phone rang. It was Wid Matthews, the Cubs general manager. He said, 'Andy, we just made an eight-player trade with the Dodgers, and you're part of it.' My wife started to cry, that's how much we liked it in Chicago. But that's baseball, and things worked out for the best."

In Brooklyn, Pafko joined Duke Snider and Carl Furillo to form an outfield that was considered to be the best in the game at that time, and he became a footnote to baseball history.

"Not many people know that I was the left fielder when Bobby Thomson hit the home run in the left-field seats in the Polo Grounds in the third game of the playoff—the 'Shot Heard Around the World'—to win the pennant for the Giants. Later, Bobby and I were teammates with the Milwaukee Braves. Not only teammates, we were roommates. I would ask Bobby how it felt to hit that home run, and he'd say, 'Aw, Andy, that's history.' I've always said if somebody had to hit a home run to beat us out of the pennant, I'm glad it was Bobby, who's one of the nicest, and most modest, guys I've known in baseball."

Getting traded to the Braves was "a big break," said Pafko. "I finished my career in my home state of Wisconsin, and I got to play on a team that won the World Series [1957]."

For his biggest thrill, Pafko remembers a day during World War II when he was playing for the Los Angeles Angels in the Pacific Coast League. "My idol when I was a kid was Joe DiMaggio," said Pafko, "and he was stationed in California. One night, he came to the game, and when he walked into the ballpark, I thought I had died and gone to heaven. Later, I had my picture taken with him and he put his arm around me and said, 'Kid'—that's what he called me, 'kid'—he said, 'Kid, I'll see you in the big leagues.'

"A couple of years later, I made the All-Star team and the game was in Chicago. I was the starting center fielder for the National League, and DiMaggio was the starting center fielder for the American League. There I was, on the same field and playing the same position as my idol."

The deal was a shocker. Borowy was only 29 and was considered a future ace for the Yankees. He had won 46 games in his first three seasons and was 10–5 at the time of the trade. But with the Yankees going nowhere in the American League and facing a roster problem, Borowy was placed on waivers. The Yankees figured he would be passed by every other team and clear waivers. Fourteen teams did pass on him, but the Cubs swooped in and claimed him.

Borowy proved to be the missing piece to the Cubs' pennant puzzle. He won 11 of his 13 decisions in Chicago—including three victories over the

The last World Series game to be played in Wrigley Field was Game 7 against the Detroit Tigers in 1945. The Tigers won 9–3, winning the Series four games to three. *Photo courtesy of Getty Images.*

rival Cardinals—posted an earned run average of 2.13, and insured the Cubs their first pennant in seven years.

Borowy started Game 1 of the 1945 World Series against the Tigers and their ace, Hal Newhouser, the American League MVP. Borowy went all the way on a six-hitter in a 9–0 victory. The Tigers evened the Series by winning Game 2, but Passeau pitched a one-hitter (a third-inning single by Rudy York) to win the third game, 3–0.

Again, the Tigers came back to take Game 4 and then won Game 5, 8–4, as Newhouser defeated Borowy, who came back the next day to pitch four innings in relief in a 12-inning, 8–7 Cubs victory that sent the Series to a sudden-death seventh game.

Borowy got the start in Game 7, pitching with only one day of rest, but was driven out in the first inning, and the Cubs were again denied a chance to win their third World Series, for which they had been waiting 37 years. They're still waiting.

I know about the 1932 Cubs and the 1935 Cubs that won 100 games and the 1938 Cubs with the famous "homer in the gloamin'" by Gabby Hartnett—they're all pennant winners. But once again I'm going to exercise my prerogative and select the **2003** squad as the fifth-best team in Cubs history. My reason is that I believe this team's success, which was so unexpected, ushered in a new era in Cubs history that will, some day soon, result in the team's first World Series championship in almost 100 years.

Dusty Baker took over as manager, improved the team by a remarkable 21 games, and won the team's first division championship, by one game over Houston in the National League Central. Sammy Sosa hit 40 home runs, giving him a National League record of six straight years with at least 40 homers, and drove in 103 runs for another NL record, nine straight years with at least 100 RBIs. Kerry Wood and Mark Prior were first and second in the league in strikeouts, and the Cubs came five outs away from going to the World Series for the first time in 58 years.

I'll get to that sad story in a bit. But first, the good stuff. After winning the NL Central, the Cubs met the Atlanta Braves, who had won 101 games and their 12th-straight NL East title. The Braves were heavy favorites to knock the Cubs out of the playoffs. But Wood and Prior dominated in the five-game division series.

With Prior (top), Sosa, and others leading the charge, the 2003 Cubs were within five outs of the World Series before the cheers unbelievably turned to tears. *Photos courtesy of AP/Wide World Photos.*

Kerry pitched 7⅓ innings in the first game, allowed just two hits, struck out 11, and beat the Braves 4–2. After Atlanta won Game 2, Prior pitched a complete game two-hitter, struck out seven, and beat the Braves and Greg Maddux 3–1.

What would have happened if the fan (I won't mention his name—the guy has suffered enough grief) had not touched the ball? Would the Cubs have gone on to win the game, advanced to the World Series, and ended almost 100 years of suffering? We'll never know.

The Braves won Game 4, and that left it up to Wood in Game 5. Again, Kerry came up big: eight innings, five hits, and seven strikeouts for a 5–1 win. The Cubs had won a postseason series for the first time since 1908, and were on their way to the National League Championship Series for the first time since 1989.

Their opponents in the NLCS were the Florida Marlins, the wild-card team that had shocked the Giants to advance to the finals, and the matchup produced an exciting—and frustrating (for the Cubs)—high-scoring seven games.

In Game 1 Florida pounded out 14 hits, slugged four homers, and outscored the Cubs 9–8 in 11 innings. The Cubs counted on Prior to stop the bleeding in Game 2, and he came through with seven solid innings for a 12–3 victory to tie the series 1–1.

Game 3 was another 11-inning marathon, but this time the Cubs prevailed 5–4 on Doug Glanville's pinch-hit RBI triple.

In the fourth game Aramis Ramirez belted a grand slam in the first inning and later drove in a fifth run with a single and a sixth with a solo homer. The Cubs won 8–3 to go up, three games to one, just one win away from reaching the World Series and with three games to get there.

The Marlins kept their hopes alive with Josh Beckett's complete game, 11-strikeout two-hitter to win Game 5 4–0, but despite the loss, the Cubs had the satisfaction of knowing that the game or games would be played at Wrigley Field, where the home fans could share in the joy of seeing their Cubs advance to the World Series.

The excitement at Wrigley was high in Game 6 as the Cubs put up single runs in the first, sixth, and seventh innings. Prior pitched brilliantly, allowing no runs and three hits (all singles) over seven innings. Then came that fatal eighth inning.

With one out, Juan Pierre slapped a double down the left-field line. The next batter, Luis Castillo, hit a lazy foul fly ball to left. Cubs left fielder Moises

Alou was poised under it, ready to make the catch for the second out, when a fan reached out and deflected the ball. Alou was livid. He swore he would have made the catch, and I agree.

What would have happened if the fan (I won't mention his name—the guy has suffered enough grief) had not touched the ball? Would the Cubs have gone on to win the game, advanced to the World Series, and ended almost 100 years of suffering? We'll never know.

What we do know is that Castillo walked, Pudge Rodriguez followed with an RBI single, and the carnage was on. When it ended, the Marlins had scored eight runs for an 8–3 victory that forced a Game 7.

The Cubs tried to put up a brave front, confident because they had their ace, Kerry Wood, rested and ready for the sudden-death seventh game. But you could tell the Cubs were deflated—and the Marlins were energized—by what happened in the eighth inning of Game 6.

The Marlins reached Wood for three runs in the first, but the Cubs showed some fight by coming back with three in the second and two in the third for a 5–3 lead. The Marlins also had some fight left in them. They regained the lead with three in the fifth, added one in the sixth, and had two in the seventh for a 9–6 victory.

The Marlins went on to beat the Yankees in the World Series and, naturally, Cubs fans had to wonder: if they had beaten the Marlins, could they have beaten the Yankees and ended their World Series drought? Again, we'll never know.

Of all the disappointments and frustrations that the Cubs and their fans have suffered over the years, losing to the Marlins in the 2003 National League Championship Series—and the heartbreaking way they lost—might have been the worst. But I am, and always have been, a positive guy, and I say that the pain of that eighth inning of Game 6 of the National League Championship Series in 2003—and all the rest of the suffering over the last century—will only make it that much sweeter when the Cubs finally win the World Series. I believe they *will* win the World Series, and they'll do it soon.

Statistical Summaries

TEAM STATISTICS

W = Games won

L = Games lost

PCT = Winning percentage

GA/B = Games ahead/behind

RS = Runs scored

RA = Runs allowed

BA = Team batting average

HR = Home runs

ERA = Team earned run average

Year	W	L	PCT	GA/B	RS	RA	BA	HR	ERA
1969	92	70	.568	-8	720	611	.253	142	3.34
1906	116	36	.763	+20	704	381	.262	15	1.75
1929	98	54	.645	+10.5	982	758	.303	139	4.16
1945	98	56	.636	+3	735	532	.277	57	2.98
2003	88	74	.543	+1	724	683	.259	172	3.83

Index

Entries in italics denote references to photo captions.

Aaron, Henry "Hank," 34, 16
Adams, Franklin P., 34, 52
Adams, Sparky, 102
African Americans. *See* Chicago Cubs: racial integration; racial discrimination; racial integration
Agee, Tommie, 125, 167
Alexander, Grover Cleveland, 1, 129, 173
Allen, Dick, 126
All-Star Game, 3, 5, 21, 67, 102
Alou, Felipe, *74*, 75–76
Alou, Jesus, 75
Alou, Matty, 75
Alou, Moises, 69, *74*, 75–76, 79, 80, 180–81
Amalfitano, Joey, 125
American Association, 65
American Monthly, 113
Andujar, Joaquin, 140
Anson, Adrian "Cap," 16–20, *17*, 25, 26, 65, 149, 155–57, *156*, 163
Archer, Jimmy, 9
Atlanta Braves, 141
    Greg Maddux, 115
    trades, 6, 7
    vs. Cubs in 2003 playoffs, 178, 180

Baker, Dusty, 149, 157, 157–58, 163, 178
Baker, Frank "Home Run," 63
Baltimore Orioles, 142, 145
Banks, Ernie, 1, 13–16, *14*, 25, 26, 43–44, *44*, 55, 56, 63, 71, 91, 165, *168*
base stealing, early use of, 156
Baseball Hall of Fame. *See* National Baseball Hall of Fame
"Baseball's Sad Lexicon" (Adams), 34, 51–52
Beckert, Glenn "Beck," 4, 31–34, *33*, 41, 124, 153
Beckett, Josh, 180
Bench, Johnny, 2, 11, 71, 124
Benitez, Armando, 139

Berra, Yogi, 2, 10
Berryhill, Damon, 6
Blue, Vida, 127
Borowy, Hank, 174, 175, 177–78
Boston Braves, 36, 161
    trades, 37
Boston Herald, 45
Boston Red Sox, 6, 23–24, 83, 98, 99, 113
    last to break color barrier, 48
    trades, 142
    vs. Cubs in 1918 World Series, 131
Boswell, Ken, 167
Boudreau, Lou, 154, 158
Bowa, Larry, 29
Boyer, Ken, 63
Branca, Ralph, 85–86, 151–52
Braves Field, 45
Bresnahan, Roger, 10
Brett, George, 63
Bridwell, Al, 36
Brock, Lou, 4, 89
Broglio, Ernie, 4, 89
Brooklyn Dodgers, *10*, 83, 99, 174. *See also* Los Angeles Dodgers
    Leo Durocher as manager of, 151–52
    trades, 1, 52, 84, 85, 103, 133, 176
    vs. Giants in 1951 NL championship, 85–86
Brown, Mordecai "Three-Finger," 109, 113–15, *114*, 120, 121, 169
Buckner, Bill, 23–24, *24*, 26
Buhl, Bob, 111
Bush, Donie, 103
Bush, Guy, 47
Bush, "Bullet" Joe, 131

Campanella, Roy, 2, 3
Carey, Max, 103
Carreon, Camilo, 125
Casey, Hugh, 133
Castillo, Luis, 180–81
Cavarretta, Phil, 18–19, 20–23, *21*, 25, 26, 174, 175
Chance, Frank, 34, 36, 51, 169, *170*
Chandler, Happy, 151

Chase, Hal, 129
Chicago Cubs
    fan interference, 180–81
    fans, 57, 64, 96, 102, *173*
    media coverage, 15
    racial integration, 15, 156
    retired player numbers, 16
Chicago Whales, 52
Chicago White Sox, 3, 20, 36
    trades, 69, 95, 125
    vs. Cubs in 1906 World Series, *133*, 169, 170
Chicago White Stockings, 20, 62, 65, 105, *See also* Chicago Cubs
Cincinnati Reds, 113, 124, 129, 142
    trades, 52, 75
    vs. Cubs in 1917 double no-hitter, 129–30
    vs. Cubs in Holtzman's 1971 no-hitter, 124
Clendenon, Donn, 167
Cleveland Indians, 125, 131
Cobb, Ty, 9
Cochrane, Mickey, 2, *21*, 174
Colavito, Rocky, 125
Collins, Jimmy, 63
Collins, Ripper, 21
Concepcion, Dave, 124
Cordero, Francisco, 139
Cronin, Joe, 3
Cubs' Fantasy Camp, 7
Cubs Park. *See* Wrigley Field
Cuyler, Kiki, 77, *78*, 83–84, 95, 100, *102*, 102–5, 107, 173–74
Cy Young Award, 112, 115, 119, 140

Dalrymple, Abner, 20
Davis, Jody, 1, 6, 7, *8*, 12
Dawson, Andre "the Hawk," 95, 96, 98–99, *100,* 106, 107
DeJesus, Ivan, 29
Derringer, Paul, 174, 175
Detroit Tigers, 2, 10, 22
    vs. Cubs in 1907 World Series, 115, 170
    vs. Cubs in 1908 World Series, 115
    vs. Cubs in 1945 World Series, 21, *177,* 178
Dickey, Bill, 2
DiMaggio, Joe, 175, 176
Dodger Stadium, 87
Dominican Republic, 76, 96

Dreyfuss, Barney, 103
Duffy, Hugh, 3
Dunston, Shawon, 19, 43, *53*, 53–54, 56
Durham, Leon "Bull," 141
Durocher, Leo "the Lip," 29, *32*, 51, 57, 63, 111, 149–53, *150*, 162, 166–67

Ebbets Field, 85
Eckersley, Dennis, 139
Eilbach, Lee, 125
Ellsworth, Dick, 123, *130*, 131, 135, 136, 146
Elston, Don, 137, *145*, 145–46, 148
English, Woody, 46, 57, 66, *66*, 68
ESPN, 119
Evers, Johnny "the Crab," 34–37, 35, 41, 169, *170*

Federal League, 52
Feller, Bob, 175
Fingers, Rollie, 137, 139
Fisk, Carlton, 2
Flint, Silver, 10
Flood, Curt, 48, 52
Florida Marlins, 98
    vs. Cubs in 2003 NL Championship Series, 61, 180–81
Foster, George, 124
Foulke, Keith, 139
Foxx, Jimmie, 3, 18, 81, 174
free agency, 109
    Andre Dawson and, 98, 99
    Rick Monday, first player drafted with, 88
French, Larry, 123, 131–34, *132*, 136
Frey, Jim, 6, 119
Furillo, Carl, 84, 176

Gagne, Eric, 137, 138, 139
Gallagher and Shean, 160
Garagiola, Joe, 18
Garrett, Wayne, 167
Gashouse Gang, 37, 153
Gehrig, Lou, 3, 81
Gentry, Gary, 167
Gernert, Dick, 155
Gibson, Bob, 71
Glanville, Doug, 180
Glavine, Tom, 126
Gold Glove Award, 5, 23, 27, 30, 43, 62, 96, 98, 115
Gossage, Goose, 137, 139

Grace, Mark, 19, *22*, 23, 26
Green, Dallas, 29
Green, Pumpsie, 48
Greenberg, Hank, 18
Grimes, Burleigh, 57, 84, 129
Grimm, Charlie, 3, 38, 47, 59, 84, *132*,
    149, 158–61, *159*, 163, 174
Grove, Lefty, 174

Hack, Stan, 19, 57–59, *58*, 66, 67, 68, 174,
    175
Hackenschmidt, George, 83
Hands, Bill, 4
Hartnett, Charles Leo "Gabby," 1–4, *2*, 7,
    8, 11, 12, 160, 178
Harwell, Ernie, 10
Henrich, Tommy, 133
Henry, Bill, 146
Herman, Billy, 29–31, *32*, 40, 41, 48
Hickman, Jim, 166, *166*
hit-and-run play, early use of, 156
Hoffman, Trevor, 139
Holland, John, 158
Hollocher, Charlie, 1
Holtzman, Kenny, 88, 123–27, *124*, 135,
    136, 166
"homer in the gloamin'," 3, 4, 178
Hornsby, Rogers, 37–39, 41, 69, *90*, 160,
    172, 173–74
Houston Astros, 61, 118, 127, 178
Houston Colt .45s, 72. *See also* Houston
    Astros
Hrniak, Walt, 18
Hubbell, Carl, 3, 131
Hubbs, Kenny, 34
Hundley, Randy "Rebel," 1, 4–5, *5*, 7, 11,
    12, 63, 64, 165
Hunter, Catfish, 111, 127

International League, 155
Isringhausen, Jason, 139

Jackson, Larry, 111
Jenkins, Ferguson "Fly," 59, 63, 109–13,
    110, 118, 120, 121, 165, 167
Jeter, Derek, *104*, 105
John, Tommy, 63, 125–26
Jurges, Billy, 43, 45–48, *47*, 55, 56, 66

Kaat, Jim, 139–40
Kansas City A's, 88. *See also* Oakland A's

Kansas City Monarchs, 15, 71
Kawano, Yosh, 32, 126
Kell, George, 63
Kelly, Mike "King," 95, *104*, 105, 107
Kessinger, Don "Kesh," 34, 43, 48–49, *49*,
    51, 53, 56
Kiner, Ralph, 18–19, 73, *73*
Klein, Chuck, 21, 81
Kling, Johnny, 1, 7, 9, *9*, 12, 169
Koenig, Mark, 46
Koosman, Jerry, *5*, 167
Kopf, Larry, 129
Koufax, Sandy, 123–24, *124*, 131
Kranepool, Ed, 167

Lajoie, Napoleon, 3
Lake Front Park, 20, 62, 65
Landis, Kenesaw Mountain, 82
Landrum, Don, 4
Lane Tech High School (Chicago), 18, 20
Lau, Charlie, 18
Lindstrom, Fred, 63, *132*
Lofton, Kenny, 61
Lopes, Davey, 30–31
Los Angeles Angels, 142, 176
Los Angeles Dodgers, 144–45
    trades, 6
Lowe, Bobby, 34
Lowrey, Peanuts, 75, 174
Lundgren, Carl, 169

Mack, Connie, 174
Maddux, Greg, 109, 115, *116*, 120, 121,
    180
Madlock, Bill "Mad Dog," 57, *59*, 59, 61,
    67, 68, 111
Maloney, Jim, 131
Mantle, Mickey, 16
Maranville, Rabbit, 160
Marichal, Juan, 131
Maris, Roger, 62
Marquard, Rube, 129
Marshall, Mike, 138
Mathews, Eddie, 63
Mathewson, Christy, 52, 113
Matthews, Gary "Sarge," 69, *76*, 77, 80
Matthews, Wid, 176
Mays, Carl, 131
Mays, Willie, 16, 91
Mazeroski, Bill, 31, 34
McCarthy, Joe, 2, 38, 171, 173, 174

McCarver, Tim, *88*
McCormick, Mike, 36
McDaniel, Lindy, 4
McGraw, Tug, 167
McGwire, Mark, 82, 95
McKechnie, Bill, 103
Merkle, Fred, 36
"Merkle's boner," 36
Merullo, Len, 45–46
Metkovich, George, 18
military service, 127, 133, 134, 174, 175
Miller, Hack, 83
Miller, Marvin, 52
Milwaukee Braves, 160, 161, 176
   trades, 86
Milwaukee Brewers
   trades, 131
Minnesota Twins, 53
minor leagues. *See names of individual teams*
   players who skipped, 15, 18
Miracle Mets. *See* New York Mets
Mize, Johnny, 18
Monday, Rick, 81, 87–88, *88*, 92, 93, 127
Montreal Expos, 72, 98, 99, 142
Morgan, Joe, 34
"Mr. Cub." *See* Banks, Ernie
Musial, Stan, 21, 175
Myers, Randy, 137, 142–44, *143*, 148

Nathan, Joe, 139
National Association, 17
National Baseball Hall of Fame, 3, 4, 10,
   13, 31, 63, 96, 99, 102, 105, 109, 112,
   114
National League Central championship, 6,
   178
National League championship, 58, 107
   1908, 36
   1929, 66, *102*, 103
   1932, *102*, 103
   1938, 3, 175
   1945, 59, 174, 175
   1966, 145
   1973, 10
   1984, 6, 7, 119
   2003, 61, 180–81
National League East championship, 6, *8*,
   119
National League playoffs, 152
Natural, The, 46
Neale, Greasy, 129

Negro Leagues, 71
Nehf, Art, 129
New York Evening Mail, 52
New York Giants, 75, 77, 100–101, 171
   trades, 37, 45, 48
      vs. Brooklyn Dodgers in 1951 World
         Series, 85–86, 176
      vs. Cubs in 1908 NL pennant race, 36–37
New York Globe, 52
New York Mets, 10, 22, 72, 139
      vs. Cubs in 1969 NL Championship
         Series, 153, 165–69
New York Yankees, 2, 65, 103, 142, 151,
   173
   trades, 46, 126, 174, 177
      vs. Brooklyn Dodgers in 1941 World
         Series, 133
      vs. Cubs in 1932 World Series, 46–48
Newcombe, Don, 176
Newhouser, Hal, 178
Nicholson, Bill "Swish," 21, 95, 99,
   100–102, *101*, 106, 107, 174, 175
Niekro, Phil, 124
no-hitter, James Vaughn's, 129–30
Nolan, Gary, 124
Notre Dame, 89

Oakland A's, 126, 127
O'Day, Hank, 36
Odom, Blue Moon, 127
O'Farrell, Bob, 1
Olympic Stadium, 99
O'Neill, Buck, 71
Ott, Mel, 81, 101, 152
Overall, Orval, 114, 169
Owen, Mickey, 133

Pafko, Andy, 21, 81, 84–86, *87*, 92, 93,
   174, 175–76
Passeau, Claude, 174, 175, 178
Pepitone, Joe, 153
Percival, Troy, 139
Perez, Tony, 63, 124
Pfeffer, Fred, 20
Pfiester, Jack, 123, *133*, 134, 136, 169
Philadelphia Athletics. *See also* Oakland A's
   trades, 100
      vs. Boston Braves in 1914 World Series,
         36
      vs. Cubs in 1929 World Series, *173*,
         174

Philadelphia Phillies, 75, 88, *88*
 trades, 27–29, 89, 102, 131
Pierre, Juan, 180
pitching rotation, introduction of, 156
Pittsburgh Pirates, 4, 18, 36, 59, 62,
 159–60, 170, 171, 173
 trades, 102–3, 131, 173
 vs. Brooklyn Dodgers in 1946 NL
 pennant race, 151
 vs. Cubs in 1938 NL pennant race, 3
platoons, early use of, 156
players' rights, 52
Pollett, Howard, 18, 100
Polo Grounds, 3
Prior, Mark, 178, 179, 180

Qualls, Jimmy, 168

racial discrimination, 71, 155–56
racial integration, 15, 48, 156
radio, 154, 158, 160
Raft, George, 151
Ramirez, Aramis, 57, *60*, 61–62, 67, 68,
 180
Randy Hundley's Fantasy Camp, 127
Regan, Phil "the Vulture," 137, *144*,
 144–45, 148, 165
Reitz, Ken, 141
relief pitching, 139–40
Reulbach, Ed, 7, 169
Rickles, Don, 153
Rittwage, Jim, 4
Rivera, Mariano, 137, 139
Rizzuto, Phil, 48
Roarke, Mike, 138
Roberts, Robin, 111
Robinson, Brooks, 63
Robinson, Jackie, *10*, 48
Rockne, Knute, 89
Rodriguez, Alex, 66
Rodriguez, Pudge, 181
Romano, John, 125
Root, Charlie, 47
Rose, Pete, *59*
Ruth, Babe, 3, 18, 46–47, 62, 81, 84,
 89
Ryan, Nolan, 67

St. Louis Cardinals, 9, 12, 37–38, 48, 139,
 142, 175
 trades, 57, 84, 140

 vs. Brooklyn Dodgers in 1946 NL
 pennant race, 151–52, 174
 vs. Cubs in 1946 NL pennant race, 174
San Antonio, Texas, 69
San Diego Padres
 vs. Cubs in 1984 NL Championship
 Series, 6, 7, 119
San Francisco Giants, 63
Sandberg, Ryne "Ryno," 27, *28*, 29, 30–31,
 40, 41, 98, 99
Sanderson, Scott, 119
Sanguillen, Manny, 33
Santo, Ron, 59, 62, 63–64, 155, 158, 167
 diabetes, 64, 127
Sauer, Hank, 18, 69, 73, *73*, 75, 79, 80
Schalk, Ray, 3
Scheffing, Bob, 1, 9–10, *10*, 12
Schmidt, Mike, 63
Schoendienst, Red, *5*
Schulte, Wildfire, 81, 89, 91, *91*, 93, 169
Scott, Pete, 102
Seattle Mariners, 169
Seaver, Tom, 112, 167, 168
Selee, Frank, 169–70
Shamsky, Art, 167
Sheckard, Jimmy, 169
Shibe Park, *173*
Simmons, Al, 3, 174
Simmons, Curt, 75
Sinatra, Frank, 151, 153
Slaughter, Enos, 175
Smith, Lee, 137, *141*, 141–42, 147, 148
Smith, Ozzie, 31
Snider, Duke, 84, 85, 176
Sosa, Sammy, 95–96, *97*, 106, 107, 178,
 179
Southern Association, 103–4
Southern League, 100
Spahn, Warren, 131
split-fingered fastball, development of, 138
spring training, Cap Anson's feeling about,
 156
Stanky, Eddie, 19
statistical summaries, Cubs
 of catchers, 11–12
 of center fielders, 92–93
 of first basemen, 25–26
 of individual teams, 182
 of left fielders, 79–80
 of left-handed pitchers, 135–36
 of managers, 162–63

of relief pitchers, 147–48
of right fielders, 106–7
of right-handed pitchers, 120–21
of second basemen, 40–41
of shortstops, 55–56
of third basemen, 67–68
Staub, Rusty, 72
Steinfeldt, Harry, 51, *170*
Stephenson, Riggs, 69, 77–78, *78*, 80,
 83–84, 103, 173–74
Stovey, Harry, 65
Sutcliffe, Rick, *8*, 109, *118*, 119, 121
Sutter, Bruce, 137–41, *138*, *141*, 142, 147,
 148
Swoboda, Ron, 167

Taveras, Frank, 139
Terry, Bill, 3
Texas Rangers, 59, 111
Thomson, Bobby, 85–86, 176
Thorpe, Jim, 129
Tiant, Luis, 6
Tierney, Cotton, 160
Tinker Field, 53
Tinker, Joe, 34–36, 43, *50*, 51–53, 56, 169,
 170
"Tinker-to-Evers-to-Chance," *170*. *See also*
 "Baseball's Sad Lexicon"
Todd, Al, 1
Toney, Fred, *128*, 129
Traynor, Pie, 63

University of Illinois, 125

Vaughn, James "Hippo," 123, 127–31, *128*,
 135, 136
Veeck, Bill, 57

Waitkus, Eddie, 46
Walker, Fleet, 156
Walker, Harry, 75
Waner, Lloyd "Little Poison," 103
Waner, Paul "Big Poison," 103
Waveland Avenue home runs, 16
Weeghman Park. *See* Wrigley Field
Weimer, Jake, 134
West Point, 103
Wheeler, Ralph, 45
Wilhelm, Hoyt, 139
Williams, Billy, 15, 38–39, 63, 69–72, *70*,
 79, 80, 155, 165–66, *166*

Williams, Cy, 81, 88–89, *90*, 93, 129
"Williams Shift," 89
Williams, Ted, 89, 175
Williamson, Ned, 20, 57, 62, 65, *65*, 68
Wilson, Art, 129
Wilson, Hack, 3, 18, 57, 77, *78*, 81–84, *82*,
 92, 93, 103, 173
Wilson, Jimmie, 3
Wilson, Mookie, 139
Wood, Kerry, 109, 115, *117*, 117–18, 121,
 178, 180, 181
World Series, 7, 9, 67, 103
 1906, White Sox vs. Cubs, 169, 170, *171*
 1907, Cubs vs. Tigers, 36, 114, 169, 170
 1908, Cubs vs. Tigers, 35, 36, 114, 169,
  171
 1914, Boston Braves vs. Philadelphia
  Athletics, 36
 1918, Red Sox vs. Cubs, 131
 1926, Cardinals vs. Yankees, 37
 1929, Philadelphia Athletics vs. Cubs,
  173, 174
 1932, Yankees vs. Cubs, 46–47
 1935, Tigers vs. Cubs, *21*
 1938, Yankees vs. Cubs, 35
 1941, Yankees vs. Brooklyn Dodgers,
  133
 1945, Tigers vs. Cubs, 45, 160, *177*, 178
 1957, Milwaukee Braves vs. Yankees,
  176
 1974, Oakland Athletics vs. Los Angelos
  Dodgers, 126
 1978, Yankees vs. Los Angelos Dodgers,
  126
 1986, Mets vs. Red Sox, 23
 2004, Red Sox vs. Cardinals, 131
World War II, 101, 133. *See also* military
 service
Wrigley Building, 19
Wrigley Field, 3, *21*, 33, 101, 102, 161,
 177
 flags, 16
 scoreboard, 100
Wrigley, Phil, 19
Wysc, Hank, 174, 175

York, Rudy, 178

Zimmer, Don "Popeye," 6, 149, 153–55,
 154, 162
Zimmerman, Heinie, 36